A VIEW INTO THE WORLD OF A MENTAL MEDIUM

&

THE MIND, BODY AND SPIRIT CONNECTION

By Derek Murray
Copyright Derek Murray

2019

INDEX

THAT OTHER PLACE
HELL
HOME
OWNERSHIP
WEALTH
THE GIFT
OPEN OR CLOSE
YOU
CLOSING COMMENT
THE END. (Although there is no end.)

INTRODUCTION

This book comprises two sections, the first is about mediumship and how it works for me and the second is about the connection between Mind-body-Spirit. It's now 2019, and this book has been written to reflect my current understanding. You may only have a slight interest in the subject of mediumship, or you may want to develop it, but I believe we can all connect to the nonphysical or spirit world. Some Mediums referred to their ability as a gift and in a way, it is, but it's a gift we've all been given. The thing is we don't all want to develop it. Listen to your intuition for what is right for one may not be right for another. However, you are reading this which indicates you want to take a closer look. So untie the bow and unwrapped the key that unlocks the door into a fascinating subject, and if you decided to turn the key and open the door between the two worlds, you would touch a larger truth. So take my hand and come with me as we throw the door wide open and look into another world, a world where the dragon sleeps, a world full of wonder.

A DOOR LESS OPENED

I hear voices, suffer mood swings, have images play over in my mind, plus other sensory factors such as touch, smell and pain. Oh, and I mustn't forget the added factor of feeling my body isn't my own. Mediums are individuals and connect to the unseen world in many ways. Some work in trance, or pickup audible information, others see Spirit in solid form or pick up symbols. The intention of this book is to give you a glimpse into my world, the world of a Mental Medium. The Dragon is your true spiritual self. The spiritual-self has many names, and yet no name. Some may say it is the Higher self or soul, but all names are inadequate as it's that part of you that has existed for all time and will continue to exist long after this planet has ceased to support life. It's not my intention to change your beliefs or to instruct you in a particular technique as there are many, but I will try to give insight into my method and understanding. If anyone tells you their way is the only way or if they explain with authority what the unseen world is like, they do not know, for in our present state the nonphysical world is beyond our comprehension. However, mediums are given glimpses into this other realm, but a glimpse is not the complete picture. Life is like a maze with only one entrance and one exit. There are no dead ends, and you can never turn around, but the direction you take is up to you. However, your choice will be influenced by many factors such as upbringing, social influences and strength of the ego, so the independent choice isn't as independent as first appears.

This book is split into sections, so you can jump from one to the other, or skip some altogether. I hope you find this useful and I apologize in advance if any of my views offend, that's not my intention and if they do, disregard them as being the ramblings of someone suffering an incurable illness called the human condition. Let's highlight a few facts before we go too far. I am human, therefore fallible. I know it's a sad reality, I wish it wasn't, but it's the truth. You only have to ask my wife, and she'd confirm it, sometimes I can be a complete idiot. Being a Medium does not make you superhuman or any better than anyone else, but it has helped me. I have a positive outlook on life and death. Okay death isn't something we like to talk about, but one day my body will cease to function, my heart will stop, brain shut down and the cells of my body decompose. Not a pleasant thought I know, but this is where my experience as a Medium lead me to think that we don't actually die after physical death. This is one hell of an assumption, but if you're bombarded by enough evidence logic dictates that you can't just sit back and ignore it. Being a Medium helps you see the true nature of life. Most place value on status, power, position and wealth, the development of mediumistic ability opens you to an awareness of the true values of love, empathy, understanding and happiness. Let's get that one main fact straight Mediums can be as reckless, stupid and selfish as anyone walking on this planet. From the second we were born our ego came into existence, we need it to survive, but it can end up dominating our life if we don't bring mind body and spirit into balance.

Life is not permanent, our sun will eventually go supernova, what of the human race then? All recorded history lost for eternity unless we have developed interstellar travel, but it's more likely that we will become extinct well before that. Technology may have advanced at an alarming pace, but alas humankind hasn't. We still have a long way to go. Science tries to make sense of the physical world and can now prevent people dying from diseases that only a short time ago we considered incurable, but the human race continues to commit genocide and destroy the environment. Societies develop, some change and some die, but Individuals continue to murder and commit acts that the majority find appalling, while at the same time others put their lives at risk every day of the week to keep us safe, and others work to help those who need it without the need for thanks. Putting it mildly the human family is somewhat dysfunctional. Now don't get upset or depressed, all is not lost, things may seem bad, but I want you to look inward not outward because you are an amazing individual capable of doing more than you could ever imagine. The act of developing the mediumistic ability forces you to look closely at yourself and go within, and once that door is opened, it can't be closed.

No two doors are the same, like us after time we can become worn, with a bit of damage here and there, even if we look after ourselves time will take its toll. Some doors will sparkle from being loved and cherished, but the years of cleaning will wear the surface thin. The patina of our personalities shows in our daily lives but understanding the connection between mind, body and spirit can help in practical ways. Understanding the connection between this world and the nonphysical helps in everyday life. My day job pays for all my wants and needs, so I have no need to profit from my work as a Medium. I was drawn into it and encouraged by a number of excellent practitioners and have been doing this work for many years now. Sometimes the accuracy of readings has blown me away, but not all the time, but I will get to that later, and as any genuine Medium will tell you, sometimes the connection can fall flat, or seem so.

Regardless of the reason, you have picked up this book I hope you will find enough within these pages to get you thinking. So, let's set the stage and open the door a fraction and make the Dragon stir just a little.

ONE DOOR AT A TIME

Not everyone is honest. You know it's true but let me tell you something I was told the other evening. A friend of mine was working at a Psychic supper, and it wasn't going well, whilst giving information, no one could take it. So, apologising she asked someone to take over. In stepping back, a man who works as a paranormal investigator asked why she didn't make something up? This line of work is no different to any other; some operate with the best of intentions and others don't. So remember Mediums are human and just as dysfunctional as anyone else. But why didn't it go well I hear you say? The Medium needs to be relaxed, this process is a three-way street, as all parties participating need to work together. The sitter helps by being open. However, the Medium may not be relaxed enough, or they haven't the energy required. They may be distracted, or the sitter may be negative, and that could make the Medium falter, as thinking and logic comes into play. When that happens, the reading can fall apart. Spirit can also struggle, but that's a subject that we will tackle later. The thing is that an experienced Medium keeps logic locked up and stops doubt in its tracks. Yes, the sitter may be told something they can't take or understand at the time of the reading, but maybe it could be shown to have relevance and therefore more power later. As I've already said, I'm confident we all possess some mediumistic ability. Whether you want to develop it or not is another matter, but when I hear a Medium talk about their gift, I can't help thinking they are trying to make themselves seem in some way superior. I try not to criticise others who work in this field, but we all play a part in how others perceive this ability. The media, urban myths and old wive's tales have given this subject an air of mystique when there is absolutely nothing mysterious about it. When we work between the two worlds, we have a responsibility, to be honest, and show respect to both the sitter or sitters and those in spirit. There is so much misinformation in the world that it's sometimes hard to see the truth. No one knows how the mediumistic ability works, well no one alive and kicking, and they're quite a few that say it doesn't. Now I know I am going to upset someone, but it needs to be said. 'We don't have the answers.' As much as any of us would like to think we do, we don't. The words of Socrates come to mind. 'To know is to know that you know nothing.

That is the meaning of real knowledge.' Every time a Medium stand up in front of a congregation, they need to consider what they say. I have picked up the pieces a few times. The following demonstrates in part what I mean. I was asked to undertake a reading for a colleague's wife, to which I agreed. I turned up, and before I had got over the threshold, I was shown a CD with a photo of a man on the front and asked if I knew anything about him. He was a well-known Medium and had been on television. I sensed a tension, but as I will explain later, you need to put your logic to one side. So I started and in this instance worked by producing a sketch and on handing it over the young lady went ashen. The blood just seemed to drain from her.

'You have drawn a baby! Why?'

'A baby is important.'

'Am I going to have a baby?'

'I don't know; I just know that a baby is important.'

Then she explained about the reading from the TV Medium who told her she was going to have a happy event, as she was going to have a baby, but unbeknown to him, if the young lady were to fall pregnant the result would be catastrophic as giving birth could be fatal to both mother and child. I explained that

I only saw the baby as an issue, which it was. The poor woman had been in a blind panic since that day. It didn't take long to allay her fears, but now with the passing of time, you can see how the first prediction came about, for the family is now involved in fostering very young children and babies. This takes us to the subject of prediction and prophecy an element we will go through in more detail later. This cautionary tale hopefully demonstrates the responsibility that goes with this work. Beliefs differ, and as you travel through life, you will hear many theories about the world of spirit and the reason for this or that, all of them differing. Some people are so convinced they have the truth; they cannot consider an opposing or even slightly differing viewpoint. Remain open to the possibility that what you believe to be true may be wrong. The Christian, Muslim and Jew believe their way is right, and have been at one another's throats for years, each convinced they have the answer. Even sects within groups have committed acts of atrocity against those in their faith. Any student of history can cite numerous instances where genocide has been committed under the banner of religion. The following is a quote from the Dalai Lama. 'My religion is very simple; it's kindness.' So when I work in front of a congregation or audience, I don't try to convert or convince them that I have the answer. I have a responsibility to work with spirit, and simply pass on information. I do give my opinion, but I don't package it as the truth or only path. We walk in a world that hides the truth, and today you may think one thing, then tomorrow another.

THE KEY

My subconscious influences my perception of reality, and my conscious thoughts affect not only my mental state but my physical condition as well. Studies have been undertaken that suggest certain genes can be turned on and off by the attitude of mind and thought. Science has mapped the brain and can now monitor how it functions in real time, but you and I are not just a bunch of neurons activated by trillions of electrical impulses. We are a human animal and spiritual entity capable of much more than you can imagine. From my experience as a Medium, I refute the supposition held by many, that we die completely when brain activity ceases. The majority of people walking this planet don't experience a connection from the unseen world as often as Mediums do. In this way Psychics and Mediums are privileged, but this path is made easier by help from those who've walked this way before. Having a connection over and over again is amazing, and when backed up by good validation, well that's something else as the example below shows. Psychic Suppers can be loud especially when organised as entertainment, where Mediums circulate from table to table as an added attraction to a meal and a few drinks. On this occasion, things were louder than usual as I approached my first table of the night. The five young ladies were laughing and determined to have a good night out. As I took my seat and glanced at the girl on my right, in my mind's eye, I saw a light bulb explode shattering into thousands of tiny fragments. So I smiled at her and said without my normal introduction. 'That light bulb exploding scared you half to death.' The response was of disbelief, but her main concern was the thought I'd been spying on her. However, from that moment on the laughing and joking stopped. Going to a Spiritualist church or approaching a Medium for a sitting, isn't for everyone, so Psychic Suppers play their part, and may lead those attending to look deeper. Talk to anyone working in this field, and they'll have a theory as to why and how this ability works, but all the theorising in the world won't change a thing. I have my own reasoning, but I know I'm just like a child trying to understand something beyond my grasp. All I do is accept that the process can provide amazing evidence and can bring comfort to many. However, this ability can provide much more, and the key to this is simple, in fact, I would say that the ability is an inherent part of who we are, as we are Spirit inhabiting a complex biomechanical mechanism aided by the best computer in the world, the brain. So we already possess the key, all that is needed now is to insert and turn it. One thing you need to know is that the Medium is always in charge and in control. How do I deal with the aggressive door-to-door salesman or bully who wants to force his way in? The next section explains how I prepare myself for working with spirit and how I turn the key to unlock the door.

THE SAFETY CHAIN

There are those who believe that when we vacate our bodies, we become all loving, but my experience tells of something different. When death meets us, we don't instantly cross to the world of spirit grow wings and become all-knowing. The personality doesn't instantly change, some people are kind and thoughtful, others are less so, and some are downright nasty, that's human nature. We are all different, and death doesn't change that. Books have been published about Spirit protection, and others are still waiting to be written. At the Open Circle I take I always incorporate a protective element. However, personally, I have a different approach. I know I'm protected by the most powerful element of all, stronger than faith or hope. I'm protected by love. Unconditional love cannot be broken or destroyed and is the strongest protection I could ever wish for. I will explain a little more in the next section (The Trapdoor), about trapped spirits that have not crossed over fully, but my perception is when the physical shell has been discarded, the personality, soul or spirit needs to transcend, and when I come across an earthbound spirit that hasn't moved on, I know what to do and how to do it.

Some practitioners see protection as a vital component, whilst others don't. I would be happier to think that those working between the two worlds are doing something to protect themselves rather than leaving themselves open. So, what would happen if protection was ignored? One theory is that the Medium could be overtaken by negative energy, thereby becoming drained and finding it harder than usual to function in the physical world. Every time I open myself, I'm mindful that I may attract a spirit that's not aware they no longer exist in the physical world. I will not only come into contact with spirits that will drain my energy, but people in the physical world can do that as well. Because, when I am open, I have empathy. Some try to draw my energy unintentionally, and others don't. Intense emotion is draining and working between the worlds can be exhausting and as we know if unchecked can be physically and mentally damaging. When I get into my car to take a short journey, I put my seatbelt on. I don't expect to have an accident but isn't it better to be safe than sorry? There are many methods of protection, but the one described below is the one I use.

Sitting or standing it makes no difference as long as I am comfortable because if I'm not my attention will be drawn to the discomfort and not to the task at hand. I will run through a few short visualisation exercises I've used at the Open Circle. The transcript goes like this:

I want you to relax and take a few deep breaths. You can close your eyes if you wish, (Pause). Feel the air moving in and out of your body, (Pause) in and out, (Pause). Imagine there's an orb of light floating a few feet in front of you, (Pause). It is shining with the white light of love and divine protection, (Pause). See it pulsate then slowly draw it towards you, (Pause). Visualise it penetrating your skin as it moves towards your centre, (Pause). This light shines like a beacon providing you with the most solid form of protection you could ever imagine, (Pause). Bring your awareness back to the room but keep that vision of the light shining in your core.

Spirit sees, so what I visualise and that will influence the Spirit's perception. So if a malevolent spirit comes into my area instead of seeing someone vulnerable and unsure, they see a powerful light emanating from my core. That combined with a feeling of unconditional love, creates a powerful environment for me to work in. The enemy is fear and eliminating this is the first job. The members of the Circle use their imagination and in doing so can work between both worlds. I know I'm a spirit, inhabiting a biomechanical body made of bone and sinew, and even if my body may falter nothing can harm the real me, the spirit me. other Mediums will use different visualisation exercises, some I've listed below.

THE BUBBLE. - Imagine a bubble floating in front of you, gently bring it closer so you can step into it. This bubble can only be penetrated by love. Negative energy can't get through.

MIRRORS. - Surround yourself with mirrors, making sure you are completely covered. Then any negative energy is reflected back to the person or entity sending it. I will only use this if I think an individual was not capable of handling a non-transcendent spirit at that time. (See the following paragraph.)

SHIELD OF LIGHT. – Imagine a ring of pure white light about six inches over your head.

You can put a symbol within the circle such as a cross. Then draw the light down over your body creating a protective sheath of shining white light that encapsulates your whole body. The light sheath needs to be joined under the feet and over the head.

THE CLOAK. – You need to throw the cloak of protection over you completely, not just over your shoulders but rather like Harry Potters cloak of invisibility, making sure that no part of you can be seen.

SUIT OF ARMOUR. – For this, you need to visualise yourself protected by a shining suit of polished silver. This lets nothing penetrate, and all negativity is reflected. Again, I will only use this method If I feel the individual would struggle with a non-transcendent spirit. (See the following paragraph.)

COLOUR DEFENCES. – Imagine yourself surrounded by swirling colours of white, silver or gold light. Let these colours cling to your body keeping you encapsulated.

RUNNING WATER. – Imagine running water flowing over you as if standing under a waterfall. Water is seen as a vehicle for purification, as used in the rite of baptism.

I have faith in the ability of the Circle I take, that the Rituals and visualisation exercises build a perception of protection allowing the participants to develop a skill that will assist them in understanding their true nature. However, transcended spirits understand more than we do, and would never get offended if I mistake a transcended spirit for an earthbound one. So when a spirit interacts that makes me feel oppressed or uneasy, I ask them to stand back, and the feeling subsides. Remember, what I sense, visualise and feel they also pick up and vice versa. If the connection makes me feel out of kilter, it's usually a Spirit that has not transcended, so I don't overreact, panic or push them away. I know I'm always protected and safe no matter what happens. From the connections, I've had from working as a Medium, and because of the past validation I've obtained, I understand this entity needs help. Mediumship isn't just about giving comfort to those living in the physical world; it's also about working with transcended spirits to help those in the non-physical move forward. Bearing this in mind, some of the protection exercises such as mirrors, and the suit of armour are not that helpful as the earthbound entity has the insecurity and negativity reflected back. Likewise, you will come across those who will banish nonphysical entities, but all this does is move the problem from one place to another, and the stuck spirit will be left there a little longer. Most religions see prayer, as a way of obtaining protection. The action of prayer or talking to a deity or Godhead is an everyday occurrence to some but not all. The Lord's prayer incorporates the phrase "Deliver us from evil", and the Islamic prayer for protection has in it the following: "O God I seek refuge in you from the evil in myself and every creature that you have given power over us." The process of prayer is no more than talking to the divine. Again, I state that I do not intend to cause offence to any belief system you hold, but to bring to your attention the act of praying reinforces the conscious and subconscious. Visualisation exercises I use at Circle will always include the notion of protection. Rituals can further help, but I have never used any in the Circle environment. Some Mediums will tell you that they don't bother with protection, as their guides are always there to keep them safe. That in its self is a form of protection, as their mindset is that they are being looked after. Therefore, if a malevolent entity comes along, they will see they are protected. Protection is necessary during development because the individual needs to be in control, I would also say I don't need protection because I am a spirit, but however I wish to put it, that's also a form of protection. Not all spirits act lovingly. Some haven't completed their journey from this life to the next and may not even realise they've died. I have known some who have been very abusive, which takes us to the next Chapter.

THE TRAPDOOR

Not everyone is mentally stable. There are several illnesses that manifest themselves in ways that mimic mediumistic abilities and spirit attachment. Schizophrenia is a mental disorder that manifests with hallucinations. If you've seen the film "A Beautiful Mind" released in 2001 based on the Nobel Prize winner John Nash, you will remember that John Nash was never alone and constantly had three phantom characters with him. Our minds are incredibly powerful yet fragile. I'm sure that some people who are thought to be suffering from this devastating illness are under psychic attack, while the reverse may also apply. You can understand how a disembodied spirit would react when they come across someone who is receptive. They become inquisitive and may even feel contented. When a connection is made, you may feel emotional, but the emotions may not be your own. Feelings and emotions are shared. It's not intentional, but it happens. Can a spirit take over the body of a living person? Exorcisms are still performed, so there must be some individuals who think it can. Also, one of the Mediumistic abilities is called trance (and we will tackle that in detail later.) This is when the medium lets the spirit use their body and therefore allowing direct communication to take place. I have witnessed deep trance mediumship and light trance or shadowing as it's sometimes called, and I have found it fascinating. However, some people suffer from dissociative identity disorder (DID). This is when a person displays multiple distinct identities, each one perceiving and interacting with the environment. This is classed as a psychiatric condition and a mental illness. A number of studies have been undertaken to compare this condition to mediumistic ability, and some of the studies show interesting results. Could there be a connection? The mind is a very powerful piece of equipment the biological computer that we only ever use a fraction of.

Exorcism has been going on for aeons; it's the act of driving out evil spirits. The ancient Babylonians, Egyptians and Shamans would enter an altered state in order to discover the spirit that was causing sickness and command it out, by using rituals and prayers to expel the spirit. The Church of Rome and other Christian based religions still perform the ritual of exorcism although it's less practised now. The signs of possession from the Roman ritual of exorcism are written as follows:

Firstly, the victim speaks or understands unknown languages without prior knowledge. Secondly that they know things that are distant or hidden, also that the victim can predict the future. They must show an intense hatred for holy things, and finally, they must show physical strength far above their normal condition. I don't hold the notion of casting out of evil, would you not say, that an entity in pain and torment could do with help rather than being cast out? I also have a problem with the notion of hell, to think of a place where all evil is sent, I find repugnant. In this age, many do not believe in possession except as a story, and many are afraid to think it can occur, but there are those who undertake the ritual of exorcism. I use the term ritual because that's what it is, the actions undertaken in order and with precision, in the belief that if the correct steps are taken the entity will be driven back to whence it came. Priests conducting this work need a strong faith and you couldn't but be impressed with their conviction. They feel fully protected due to their belief in their God and the divine act. The church states that possession can occur through proximity to Evil Places or Persons. Unfortunately, further comment is made, by declaring that attending spiritualistic sessions and card readers' fall into this category. The fact remains a strong belief is still held by many that demonic possession is the work of the Devil. I hope that the established Christian church can one day see that what Mediums do, is in no way evil but should be embraced.

I've already stated I run an open Circle for a Spiritualist church in Worcester, and because anyone can come along, you wouldn't be surprised if someone turned up who had an issue relating to a spirit attachment. When this happens, I have a rule that I will help, firstly because you don't want any disruption during the Circle and secondly because it's of interest to the rest of the group. Some attend because they are inquisitive while others are looking to develop their abilities. However, regardless of the reason, there is a need to understand that taking this road in ignorance isn't wise. I've been helped along the way by spiritualists and Mediums who I will always hold in high regard, but as the knowledge is passed on through the ages, the information is seen differently by subsequent generations. I would love to experience what is understood about this subject in another two thousand years. I think that some Mediums work with guides and helpers, that haven't transcended.

I will recount an incident that happened when I attended a circle. The lady taking it was standing in for the usual Medium. She seemed positive and kept referring to her guides, talking to them as if they were standing just behind her. A man who had been going to this circle for a few weeks was sitting relaxed in his chair with his legs outstretched. She snapped, "Sit up straight and uncross your legs". He explained he was more comfortable in that position, but she snapped again. I could sense his embarrassment, so I spoke up "Come on mate go easy on him!" Why I used the term "mate" at the time didn't dawn on me seeing as I was addressing a lady, but she instantly turned on me and hissed each word slowly through her teeth. "I am no mate of yours." It wasn't her voice it was the voice of a man. Her eyes were wide and piercing, then instantly she turned back and continued working as if nothing had happened. The man excused himself and left the circle, but I stayed, intrigued to discover what had happened. The lady who was taking the circle spoke to me afterwards, and from the conversation, I was certain that she'd no idea that the incident had happened. Although I try not to criticize my fellow Mediums, some run the risk of getting into deep trouble, one I know channelled an old man without warning. His voice faltered as panic set in. He was incontinent and frightened. While the evening finished okay, the Medium hasn't worked the platform since, and now only undertakes telephone readings. It's a shame, but I think I understand why. He always talked about his guide, a young man, but there were a few references about his guide swearing and being disrespectful. That I now understand are the attributes of a spirit that hasn't transcended. However, I am no better, as the next paragraph demonstrates.

She appeared, dressed in white, and holding two short swords, one in each hand. The young Japanese lady held her gaze down in a timid manner, offering me both swords. Appearing many times over the years, I believed her to be a guide and helper. She would often appear whilst I was meditating, offering me the swords and smiling. Why I thought she was a guide, I can't recall, but that's what I believed, up until the penny dropped. Because I was already involved with rescue work, I'm surprised by the situation I am describing. One night, I had a particularly bad evening as a Medium. It started reasonably well but ended with a performance that was less than impressive.

Later that same night the Japanese lady appeared. I don't know what made me realise, but suddenly it dawned on me, she hadn't fully crossed. For years, I had been comfortable in her company. I, of all people, couldn't be mistaken, could I? Anyway, I took the time to sit quietly and open myself. Immediately she appeared. I welcomed her and asked her to sit and take tea. As we sat, I started to change things. I made the tea house where we sat brighter and surrounded it with a pretty Japanese styled garden. I changed the appearance of her kimono from white, to white with large red flowers. I continued to make the surroundings more colourful. Then I constructed a meandering path leading from the teahouse to the other side of the garden, where a bridge had appeared. I could immediately make out a person on the bridge. I directed her attention to the pathway and the person waiting. We never communicated with words and this was no different, her look said it all as she slowly rose, walked along the path, stopping briefly to wave and smile, then continued to walk on, never looking back. She was greeted on the bridge and faded out of sight. The picture in my mind dissolved and I knew she was now in a place where she could progress. At the same time, I felt a little sad, for she had become attached to me and I to her. This illustrates how easy it is to be fooled.

When death comes, some people don't cross over or transcend as they should, sometimes it can be through fear, or as in this next example from not grasping they have taken their final breath. To them, they are still dealing with the issues that were occurring at the time of their passing.

The next account helps to illustrate this. But forgive the use of colourful language as I've taken the liberty of writing this from the perspective of the trapped spirit. This rescue caught my attention as one of the ladies of the Circle went into a trance. It was a bit odd as the lady in question is very proper and what came out of her mouth was a bit of a shock. The first we knew of it was when she said in a gruff voice 'Bastards, bloody bastards.'

To some death is a painful experience having part of your body blown apart. Although yet I've not seen the effects of gas, I've heard the stories of men dying in agony. Poor bastards, it turns my stomach just thinking about it. Some are luckier, a bullet through the skull. That's if you are stupid enough to stick your head over the top, or unlucky enough to be blown apart by a neatly aimed mortar. Unless you've experienced life in this godforsaken hellhole, it's difficult to grasp. You have heard stories but let me tell you nothing can prepare you for living in this place. Shells and sniper bullets are a constant worry. The mud makes life miserable enough, without being concerned about getting your brains blown out. My mates are falling fast. It was my choice to make the army my profession. I am proud of my position and place in the order of things. But out here it's become a case of the blind leading the blind. Things are getting out of hand, with commissioned officers being pushed through the system so quickly that a Tommy just out of basic training knows as much. If it weren't for the few experienced men like me, it would be utterly hopeless. You don't like to show your shit scared, when you're standing at the side of a lad who only a few weeks ago hadn't been outside his village, but no matter what you say or do it wouldn't make the slightest difference. We have been building up to this moment for days, and now the time has come. Each and every man coiled tight like a spring just waiting to go over. Each one knows what lies ahead. "Come on son stick close, and you'll be OK," That's all I can think to say. Not much, at a time such as this, but it was better than silence. The waiting was bad. If you forgot about the war and just concentrated on the day-to-day issues like hygiene, or the lack of it. Lice, fleas and mud were a constant problem, but now all that seemed preferable to what was ahead. The scaling ladders were in place, and we were ready. The time was set, our big guns opened from behind, it was as if all that pent-up fear had been let loose at once. "Get ready, five minutes to go", said the commander in a convincing manner. This felt like the longest five minutes of my life. Then the whistle blew, and before you could say, Jack Robinson, we were over the top. Chaos and carnage everywhere, but we moved as one. The wire cutting party had done a good job earlier. You couldn't even hear yourself think. Fritz was responding with shells and rapid gunfire. We made good headway despite the shrapnel, barbed wire and mud. The young lad who had been by my side earlier was nowhere in sight. I stumbled and fell and lost my grip on my rifle for a second, but I was soon up and going as fast as I could. I didn't pay much heed when I saw a man fall, but it did hit me when I heard a pained voice cry 'Help me, help me please'. The best we could do would be to get across then go back and help the poor buggers left behind. I didn't see the hole in front of me till I fell in it. One moment I am side by side with my comrades, with shells landing all around making the air thick with a smell of cordite, death and fear. Then the next second, time seems to stand still and I'm lying in the mud with a bayonet being drawn out of my side. Fritz is standing above me looking more scared than a Fox caught by the hounds. What happened next was weird, very weird. It just went quiet as all the shouting and gunfire stopped. Had we been so overrun? I knew where I was, with Jerry just waiting. The smoke and mist were thick, and I dare not make a sound otherwise, another bastard with a bayonet would come along to finish me off. I knew that Jerry's trench wasn't far away. When you're as near as that to the enemy, you try not to make a noise. Now that's quite difficult when your innards have just been shredded. I passed out a few times because I had vivid dreams of home, the open field where I walked as a lad and the parade ground. I could see as clear as day, my mum on her hands and knees scrubbing the front step. I would swear that it was a competition between aunty Doris two doors up. No contest, mum would win every time. She loved Doris without a doubt, but mum loved everyone. Then I could see the open fields that my brother and I played in. God, I missed him and after he died mum was never fully the same again. Just sixteen and he looked so fit and healthy, but you can't see what lurks inside. The doctors said that nothing could be done even if they had known. It seemed that he'd have his whole life before him, and then he just suddenly collapsed and died. I thought I caught sight of him, as he was all those years ago, running across the far field waving. Then the next thing I was standing next to my billet facing the parade ground. I enjoyed every second of life back then. There was an order to things everyone knew where they stood. Literally. "Fancy, seeing you," someone said. "I thought you would have lasted much longer". As I turned to see who it was, I regained consciousness and found myself back just a few feet from Jerry and literally petrified. I couldn't move, but on the plus side, I didn't want to move either. What the hell was this war about? Kill or be killed. I am a fighter in the true sense of the word professionally as well as in attitude, one of the best, how many have I killed? More than my share, that's for sure. That bastard sneaking up on me like that, he must be close. I can sense these things! The pain from my side didn't hurt as much as it should. If I could get to the medics quickly, I would be in with a chance. 'Bastards, bloody bastards.' I cursed under my breath. But I mustn't make a noise. Christ I could do with a fag, but if I had one, I couldn't light it, to close to Jerry. It felt like time was being drawn out. It's at this point that I make up my mind to try and get back. It was bloody obvious that if I didn't get moving and do something soon, I would be dead before long. I knew that the mist was not going to clear quickly, I couldn't see more than a few feet in front of me, but those bastards couldn't see me either. God, it was slow going. My jacket was doing a good job of holding my innards together. Or maybe the wound wasn't that bad, but something was stopping my guts from spilling over the floor. I had to stop and rest for a while, not long but just long enough to get my strength. God, I was so tired. I closed my eyes. I must be worse than I think I am because I'm hallucinating. I can hear and see a group of people just up in front of me. Why would people dressed in civvies be out here? They are telling this little girl she shouldn't be afraid. I am hallucinating. I must be, or I'm going round the bend? Could be both. The little girl is on the floor playing with some toys. Now more children are joining in. She seems a lot happier, and then she just ups and leaves with the other children. What was going on? Here we are in no-mans-land, and I can see this little group sitting in a circle. It's though I am standing behind one of the ladies. I can feel the calm. Now I am completely entranced. They are sitting like statues. One person says that they have a man dressed in uniform standing in front of her. She describes him, but I don't see anyone else. Come to think of it all these people seem to be dressed oddly! I can't see this soldier that is being talked about. She says he's just waiting. Suddenly I am back in the real world with the smell and the mist. Fear just overwhelms me. I can't see a bloody thing, but I know if I don't get moving soon, I'm a goner. The next second, I'm even closer to this lady, and I feel as if I am sitting in this circle. All the sensations I feel are different. The mist has gone, and I speak aloud. 'Bastards, bloody bastards.' I heard myself, as clear as day as I said again. 'Those bloody bastards with bayonets.' Then someone spoke to me; it didn't make sense, well not at first. Saying not to be worried. It's all right for someone to tell you not to worry when they're not the one with their innards waiting to spill out over the floor. They told me that the wound was healed and that my uniform was no longer dirty, torn or bloody. I panicked, especially when they told me I was dead. Then they said that I was no longer in danger, warm, dry, and without pain. It made no sense I felt very much alive. How could I be dead? Dead is dead I've seen enough death on the battlefield to know what death looked like. Then as I looked down, I saw my uniform it looked like new and the buttons so bright. They asked me if I could see another soldier standing nearby, then for the first time, I could make out the hazy outline of someone standing a short distance from me. Then I realised it was the soldier that the other person said was waiting. I knew he was one of ours, but I didn't recognise the uniform. He saluted and smiled. I knew he was OK. He patted me on the back as we started to walk away slowly from the group, and as we did, I could see some of my mates waving, trying to get my attention. To say I felt good was an understatement. The soldier who was with me turned to the small group and waved back. It was as if he knew them well. Then my mates just swamped me shaking my hand, patting me on the back and generally all talking to me at the same time. A few I knew had fallen weeks before, one shot through the head taking half of his face off. Not a scratch on him now and I'm sure he looked younger, with more hair.

The reason for writing that story from the perspective of the trapped soldier is because it's hard to explain the dynamics of a rescue Circle, but I will try. The Circle works as a cohesive unit, like a flock of birds twisting and turning, each making a connection, getting a feeling or impression and conveying it to the rest. This builds a picture that the group can work with. Emotions, visions and sensations bring clarity. If you watch any television programme featuring Mediums, they usually see the spirit in solid form, and it's true some do, but that's not always the case. I feel the spirit, as if I am them, I know what they think it's like I can access their memory. I understand why they feel the way they do. This gives me empathy as I get impressions, mental images and their pain. One thing you can guarantee the connection is always highly charged and emotional. Rescue Work is rewarding although verification is nearly always impossible. This work is considered foolhardy by some, and the height of stupidity by others but I hope that this will give some recognition to those who undertake this work. The dynamics of Rescue work are hard to explain, but empathy is a very important element, even if the entity is less than friendly, as in the next example.

This connection manifested itself through a trance state where the Medium is not always aware of their actions. The entity in a way inhabits their body and is able to use the Mediums voice.

He was miserable. No, that's an understatement! He was miserable and ill-tempered. During his life, the only thing that mattered was money. He thought that it would give him power, and from that, happiness. He was ruthless in his business. He'd gathered around him all the trappings of a wealthy man, and he found pleasure in making others feel uncomfortable. He wanted to remain top dog, thinking power and wealth brought true friendship and happiness. The first the Circle became aware of him was when one of the members picked up a sense of moaning and groaning and a feeling of being in a state of limbo. I explained that his physical body was dead, and he could now progress to the next stage, but he didn't want to move on. Maybe held back by fear of what could be waiting. Then one of the Circle spoke her voice was clipped and harsh. He felt he was being tormented because of his past deeds. When he was alive he was feared and hated by those close to him; they laughed when he laughed but not from within. They only joined in to remain in their positions, being afraid of the consequences if they didn't. He kept repeating that no one ever liked him. I told him that no one walking this planet is perfect. I let him know that I understood, as I had done things, I wasn't proud of. I explained, no one would pass judgment on him, I asked what he really wanted during his life. Then his voice faltered as he said. 'All I ever wanted was to be loved.' 'But you didn't know how to be.' I responded. 'You were never shown.'

I continued to tell him I didn't think him wholly responsible, as he was never shown love, so how could he ever give it? He spoke of a time when he was shown love; all be it for a short period when he was a child. She was elderly and had looked after him till she passed away leaving him to fend for himself. We all visualised an elderly lady standing in the centre of the circle. I explained that there were helpers waiting to assist him. I asked if he could see anyone standing nearby. We knew he had spotted her as immediately the atmosphere changed. The overwhelming sense of forgiveness and understanding could not be denied. Then once again we were left sitting as before in our small circle. The connection severed.

My brain is a fragile and complex mechanism the same as yours, but to work as a Medium, I need to place my logical mind to one side. My job is to work with the spirit world; it may be to pass on information or to help some poorly lost soul. The work is important, but it's not for everybody. I need to feel empathy for the person in front of me, and making them feel at ease is important, but to do this work well, I need to forget logic. My brain is the hardware and my thought process the software and requires constant upgrading to recognise the difference between a trapped spirit, a spirit that is in the process of transcending and one that has transcended.

THE DOOR WITHIN A DOOR

Some days I can fly high, then the next I crash. Why? The answer's simple. I'm not perfect. Sometimes I get in the way, sometimes I'm not relaxed, and sometimes I'm just not in the right frame of mind, or to be more precise I start thinking instead of being in a place between thought. There is no ritual or magical incantation, the process is simple, relax, don't even think, just relax. That's easier said than done I know, but this is how I manage to do it. I sit, not with my legs crossed in the lotus position, but comfortably, being aware of my body. I say a short prayer, not directed at God but at Spirit. In a form, like the one I will offer prior to the start of a Circle. It goes like this:

Divine Spirit; help me draw the two worlds closer together.

Enable me to receive clear and positive information.

Surround me with the white light of love and protection and bless what I do, as all I do I do in the name of love.

As I say the words 'Surround me with the white light of love and protection.' I visualise a bright light shining from my very core. I forget logic and reason and concentrate on the feelings and sensations that happen between thought. This is a tricky element to describe so bear with me. The other evening I had the feeling that my arm was limp and my hand twisted, this wasn't a conscious thought for at the time I was trying to encourage others to explain the sensations they were getting. So suddenly feeling that way was a bit of a shock. The connection happened without me trying to make it happen, as I was actually concentrating on something else. At the same time, I knew I was a young man or boy, but the point is that I wasn't thinking about it. So I was sitting relaxed, and I've offered my prayer. Now what, I hear you say. That's it. There is nothing else. I can't make my mind blank. Ask anyone to imagine nothing and they can't, the brain cannot stop working, and thoughts will come and go. I am now an interpreter explaining what I am getting. When I started developing this ability, I thought it was just my imagination, and in a way, it is, but I am allowing the Spirit to use my frame of reference. Spirit is interacting with Spirit one with a physical body and one without. It's that simple. It has taken years to develop this simple ability and sometimes it's less effective than others, but each time I open myself, it can be one hell of a ride. I experience all the emotions and sensations of Spirit, and likewise, they will be picking up my emotions. There are many ways to help someone to open, and the following paragraph will detail some I use in the Development Circle.

A Development Circle would probably start with a prayer, then a relaxation exercise. There are many, but how you relax is unimportant, but with the practice of Mental Mediumship, relaxation is the key. If you are not relaxed, it won't happen.

I've often used an exercise in a Development Circle where I direct attention to each section of the body, starting with the toes, making those in the Circle wiggle them and relax them. Then I move to the feet making them aware of all the tendons and relaxing them. The Circle will follow through each section. I will repeat the word 'relax' over and over again. Each section is tackled in turn from the toes up to the shoulders, and then I work on the fingers working up the arms section by section to the shoulders. At this point, we move to the neck, head and face. Then I continue with a protection exercise. Sometimes I will help them relax further by undertaking a guided meditation; this helps in forming a connection and laying a foundation.

There's no better way of gaining confidence than receiving validation, but we've all known hundreds who've passed, and many only fleetingly, also we've all done similar things, so receiving confirmation that a statement is correct isn't as straightforward as first you may think. Sometimes Spirit will give evidence not relating to the past but of what is going to happen in the near future. At the time the sitter may feel the reading hasn't gone well, but this type of reading can be the most powerful, as the following demonstrates:

I was giving a reading at a Psychic Supper when my attention was drawn towards the table number. I told the small group that the number three was significant. But my attention was drawn to it again. I couldn't seem to take my eyes off it, as the small white label with the black number three on it appeared to get bigger and bigger. I knew that a second three was also required, so I explained that two threes, not thirty-three, but two threes were critical. The whole group was looking perplexed, and no one could take it. No one lived at a number three, and three's just didn't seem to fit anywhere. So the reading on that table was marked as a definite miss. It wasn't until a few months later that I was contacted and told that although at the time, the information couldn't be taken, now it all made sense, as on the third of the month one of the group underwent medical tests, and on the third of the following month she had her results. When the sitter can take points raised, it gives an endorsement to the reading. However, the recipient gets it once, but I get it again and again. Sometimes the evidence can be so strong it seems unreal, although at the start I may think I am completely off track and not picking up what the spirit is trying to convey as this example shows.

I introduced myself to the eight young ladies at a psychic supper and gave a brief explanation of the process and how I work, then straight away I had a tremendous itching over my scalp, it was so bad I had to scratch my head. I knew this was a connection for one of the eight, although they were all looking at me as if I was completely mad. Then my lips started to tingle and sting as if burning. Again I described in detail what I was experiencing, but all I got were eight blank faces staring back at me. So with lips stinging and head itching, I continued by explaining what I saw in my mind's eye, as I sensed that under the bed was a shoebox tied with a yellow ribbon.

I described what I thought was inside, and as I did my heart sank as it was to do with the loss of a child. Still, the ladies looked blank with some shaking their heads. At this point, I thought that maybe I had got it completely wrong, and this was nothing to do with these young ladies sitting in front of me, but there comes a point where you can only hit your head against a brick wall for so long, and I was rapidly going past that. However, instead of closing the connection I continued, explaining feelings that were trapped inside. Then the pretty blond sitting on my right spoke. I had been talking nonstop for a while so when the young lady spoke all eyes went in her direction, including mine. She explained although working with the others, they were unaware she wore a wig, and although the treatment had stopped her hair hadn't grown back yet. The burning lips were a reference to an incident where Immac hair remover had been used to remove a little hair from above her lips, and the result was both painful and embarrassing. She hadn't wanted to admit the connection was for her, as she didn't want anyone to know about the wig or her condition. The other seven were sympathetic and at the same time supportive. The shoebox was as described with the ribbon and the things inside; all the items were keepsakes relating to a child. This illustrates how powerful a connection can be but getting every detail like that is not the norm. If I manage to get 80% verified, that's damn good. Now I don't beat myself up if I fall short; it's not always my fault. The sitter can sometimes be the stumbling block as the following illustrates.

Spirit can only use my experiences as a frame of reference. So it's not surprising that some aspects will not fit precisely. In nearly every reading, there will be some inaccurate information. When I was a little boy, I had a bright red pedal car. So if I get the impression of my old pedal car I may say that I've been shown a child's bright red pedal car. The sitter picks up on the pedal car but discounts it because the colour wasn't correct. The sitter usually expects the information to be precise and without error. During a service, I gave a lot of information about a man who wanted to apologise for his behaviour. I described him in detail both in looks and personality. Then I described the pub where he drank, the building looked like The Old Rectifying House a pub in Worcester, it sits by the River Severn near the bridge but there was one main difference, instead of a road between the river and the pub there was grass leading down to the water's edge, so I described what I saw. Alas, no one came forward during the service, but afterwards, a gentleman introduced himself and stated he could take everything except the name of the pub, but all the other facts fitted, spot-on. It was a shame he didn't speak up during the service, but from my standpoint, I was pretty pleased.

Another area where things can go wrong is through misdirection. I direct my efforts and attention to one person only to find later it was intended for another. This is a major failing of mine, but I'm sure I'm not the only Medium who suffers from this problem.

Sometimes I stand in front of the congregation convinced I'm in the right location, so I continue, only to find that when the reading comes to a close, the person could only verify some of the information then after the service someone tells me they could take all the points, but didn't want to interrupt thinking that the message was not for them. Another issue is that sometimes the sitter is so desperate to hear from Mum or Dad they refuse or don't recognise the old man who lived two doors down the road when they were six years old. I can't dictate who comes through and the likelihood of the sitter remembering the old man so far back is a tall order. However, regardless of all the pitfalls I continue because there is a job to be done, and after all, all I have to do is relax and let the space between thought, become my doorway into another world.

THE WRONG DOOR

It's important to do this work well and be true to the process, but this also means that I need to be aware of all the elements that can distract me in the connection. My thinking can't get in the way, and if it does, I couldn't look back with confidence and say it was just the connection, as the sitter or observers could provide information that will take me through the wrong door. It should also be noted that the sitter and observer can be influenced by the surroundings as well as me. I try to avoid undertaking a reading in the sitter's home as I could pick up unconscious clues. When I look back, I need to know I've done a good job, so this section is intended to take a close look at the main elements, the sitter or recipient, the observer, the environment and Medium. I am human, so I will have made assumptions about the recipient well before the process has started, but regardless of the reason, it is likely is that they will be in an emotionally vulnerable state. To Make assumptions about the recipient only distracts from the task. They may want to hear from a loved one or receive predictions relating to their life or the life of someone they know or may just be inquisitive, but that isn't my concern. However, as soon as I meet them information is passed from the sitter to me without a word being said. Age, sex, type and condition of clothes, the condition of skin and hands as well as physical impairments, together with their body language. Dr Desmond Morris made a reasonable living from deciphering body language. His book "The Naked Ape: A Zoologist's Study of the Human Animal" is probably his best-known work. Consider the following:

How do they stand?

Is there an indication of injury?

Do they stoop?

How do they sit?

I will pick up on facial expressions and the muscular reaction to certain statements. Then there is audible input, as the sitter or recipient will usually say something. The tone of voice can give an indication to their emotional state, and it's very difficult to prevent the recipient from volunteering any verbal information. I can tell a lot about the sitter within a few seconds and to disregard that information can be hard. The sitter will be in a state of anticipation, willing to listen and interact. This is where false memory may come into play, or the sitter can change a phrase or saying, just slightly to make it fit what they want to hear. Some Mediums will ask questions, I avoid this, I know it's rewarding to obtain validation, but there is always enough time for that when the reading is over. Any advance information however gained will engage logical thinking, and this will only erode validation. My subconscious will take these factors on board, even if I try not to let them influence me, for this reason, there is a method I employ that eliminates most if not all prior information, I've used this method at Circle a few times, I will explain the method later, but I always try to keep any contact with the sitter to a minimum. I make sure they know before I begin, so they don't think me rude, but even a smile or frown could bring my thought process into play.

I will never give a reading to someone in their own home unless others are present, purely for practical reasons, as I don't want to end up in court falsely accused of improper behaviour. I'll always ask them to have a friend with them. Observers could be classed as independent witnesses for verification, but they could also end up being the recipient. The number of observers could range from nil to hundreds, but they all play a part in the reading process. Signals can be obtained from observers just the same as with the sitter, so I will try to keep contact before and during to a minimum. Only when the reading is over can I let my guard down. The reading environment will vary, from large theatres to small intimate spaces, but if I work in a Church the size of the congregations can vary, but it's safe to assume that the congregation would hold a positive attitude towards the process, and would, therefore, be less critical. However, their desire for the information to be correct could give rise to having someone trying to make things fit.

Visiting the sitter's home for the reading gives the opportunity to pick up clues consciously or subconsciously. This will once again bring into question the validity of the reading. Information needs to be obtained independently of any known physical sense. I always scrutinize how I work because I want the reading given to stand on its own.

Some Mediums play background music, burn incense and provide subdued lighting, but one thing is necessary, all parties need to feel relaxed and comfortable. The Medium may also use tools as an aid to facilitate communication, Cards, Pendants and a myriad of other Items. Some surround themselves with these tools to give a positive subconscious impression to the sitter. I don't, what you see is what you get. When I work in front of a congregation or audience, I make sure I'm seen and heard clearly. Some in the congregation can be hard of hearing and may need a visual connection to understand. The environment can play a part, adding or subtracting to the connection, but at all times I must be free of logical thinking. This doesn't mean that I don't interact with the congregation. I have a dry sense of humour, and that can get me into trouble, as the reading can become more about the interaction between the congregation and me rather than working with Spirit. Communication always takes place in the space between thought, how and why I haven't a clue, but I've amassed substantial evidence, so I don't question, I just work with it. The wrong door is always there, and if I don't watch out, I could slip through it.

THE DOOR TO DARKNESS

I referred earlier to spirit's that hadn't progressed or transcended, and I don't think you'd be too surprised to discover that there are a number of these entities wandering around in a state of fear and torment. There are those who don't like to think about it, and many working in the spiritualist movement will not consider the possibility.

You will often hear people involved in spiritualism refer to their guides, but I wonder how many like me, and my Japanese lady are under a false assumption. When I make a connection, I become that entity; I experience what they experience, two spirits linked and intertwined. Spirit communication differs for each Medium, but when I work with a group, all the elements seem to connect making it easier to understand and work with. It is for this reason I work with a small group specialising in helping those trapped between the two worlds. When a Spirit has transcended or crossed over, they will act with understanding and kindness; they would never be abusive or be confused? They can see the bigger picture, but a stuck soul feels different. However, not every worker in this field understands that.

The Medium was giving good evidence of survival and seemed more than capable.

'I can see a young girl standing over there.' The medium said pointing to the wall behind her. 'She's very young but won't say anything."

The Medium indicated that there was a connection to someone sitting at the back, then started to describe the little girl with her lovely dress and hair in bunches. Even detailing the ball ties that held her hair. As soon as she said that, a lady that I'm acquainted with spoke up, recognising the girl and told how the child had fallen and the baubles that held her hair punctured her skull, resulting in her death. The Medium continued. 'This little girl is for you, but she's just standing there, shy, holding her head down and won't come forward. I have so many waiting so I will have to leave her and get on with the next connection'. To my surprise that's what the Medium did, I knew that the little girl needed help and as luck would have it so did the lady who recognised her, I briefly spoke with her after the service, I was relaxed, as I knew she was more than capable of doing what needed to be done being acquainted with rescue work.

Some think of scenes from the Exorcist. Whilst others are happy for the work to take place but not around them, thinking it a beacon for negativity and some question why help is needed at all, as they think the spirit realm is infallible most however just think it's scary. It's not!

THE DOOR TO CIRCLE

Circles take many forms, but all offer an environment where ideas and experiences can be shared. Thousands of people are sitting in small Circles all over the world; each will differ in form and direction, some concentrating on healing, aspects of spiritual development and mediumistic training. Each Circle treads its own path, but there are two main types, closed comprising the same people who meet regularly and open where anyone can attend. All should be run by experienced Mediums who can provide a calm and safe environment in which to work. It took me nearly forty years from my first encounter with the spiritualist movement to sitting in a Closed Circle, and I've found each encounter a stepping stone in understanding my own true self. Those who sit in Closed Circles become comfortable with each other and over time become familiar with the way each person works. This type of Circle is very rewarding. I've found through having an open mind I am able to learn a lot. As I have said, my day job pays well, so, the drive to earn money from working as a Medium has never been there. I see it more as a way of repaying, and by holding the Open Circle once a month for Blue Lodge Spiritualist Church passing on all I understand so others can benefit is reward enough. It is also a way of expressing my gratitude, plus I also continue to learn and gain insight. I am always careful about how I put the information across, making sure I give what is needed to get them on the right track. I also take on the responsibility as my actions will influence others.

THE GUIDES DOOR

I was reading an article about someone starting a circle and to their amazement, one person mentioned their guide was Rock Totem Bear, then another said that their guide was Archangel Michael, but that wasn't all, someone else mentioned they had a Warlock and just to top it all the next two had Moses. Now, maybe men in white coats should have taken them away as it all sounds a bit crazy, but this I feel needs a little explanation. Spirit can only use what resides in our conscious and subconscious mind, what has been created by our life experiences. Spirit work with our imagination, and some of us have weird stuff locked inside our heads. From my current understanding, I have many nonphysical guides and one I call Mat. So, let say it's not unusual to come across someone who thinks they have Moses or White Eagle as a guide. So, don't throw the baby out with the bathwater, Spirit will use the imagination, memories and experiences of those who have the connection, it's the message that's important, not the messenger and Spirit can only work with the tools they are given. If someone at Circle tells me, they have Queen Victoria as a guide I won't burst their bubble and who am I to say what is, or is not? The born again, Christians would say it was the love of Jesus. The Witchdoctor would say it was his ancestors. The old religion may say it's the Triple Goddess, but it's not that important how the message is delivered, it's understanding it that matters.

You may hear others talk about their guides as if they are in physical form. I don't, and thankful because if I did, I would seriously question my sanity. I am a Mental Medium because that's the direction my development has taken. My mentor, Linda Carr, was a Trance Medium. There are many theories on the subject of guides and helpers, and you could waste a lot of time contemplating the truth. But in considering the truth, you would miss the essence and the meaning. Having a guide passing the information on is possibly more acceptable to us in our current understanding. Guides and helpers also come in physical form. I've been helped by so many and appreciate all the support I've been given. The word privilege doesn't seem good enough to describe how lucky I've been. My assumption is that guides can assist but not interfere with free will, they are able to guide and provide insight but no more. In taking a Circle, I'm acting as a Guide and likewise can only give insight and assistance. With this comes responsibility, as my actions and words will influence others. I wouldn't put doubt in the mind of the person who thinks their guide is Moses, as this would be interfering. Spirit is showing its self in a way they see fit, and who's to say it's not Moses. We are like children in the presence of adults, but the guidance doesn't just come from me; I will go within and listen to that small voice of intuition, to that place between thought coming through my connection to the spirit world. I'm sure guides come and go depending on the stage of your spiritual development and needs. Remember the young Japanese lady I thought was my guide.

THE DOOR TO THE FUTURE

Can you help?

What's around the corner?

I need to know!

I am a Medium, not a Fortune Teller, but both labels are inadequate because I offer a link between this world of the physical and the nonphysical. I've heard Mediums say that they are instruments of spirit, but this makes me sound subservient, and I'm anything but. I am a spiritual being that exists in the material world. Spirit, however, has no such restrictions, they can see all possibilities with the twists and turns, and because of this, are able to help. Prediction or prophecy is tricky at the best of times. Some see the future set in stone while others see endless possibilities and there are some wacky theories floating about. Remember when I gave a reading, relating to two threes. At the time no one in the physical world knew her tests would be on the third, and the results would be received on the third of the following month, but the spirit world could see all the elements in place to make it so. Prophecy is seen as a process where the information is being provided by the divine. Fortune telling implies a more superficial form of divination, but do not think any the less of it. Tealeaf reading, Tarot, palmistry, Crystal Ball and the 'I Ching', these are just a few methods people use for divination. My mentor Linda always said that cards were for fun, but if you feel happy and relaxed using them fine. Once again, I will refer to responsibility as with every reading, and there is a risk that what I say will be misinterpreted. and misunderstood. Prediction is obscure, take the phrase. (You will lose your partner,), sounds final, but one day either my wife or I will die, so for a while, we would be lost to each other. Likewise, you would think that telling someone they were going to have a baby would be okay, but I was brought in to allay a woman's fear because another Medium had told her just that. I repeat prediction of any kind is at best obscure and at worst scary and should be treated with caution.

I will make three predictions; I'm going to expire, this planet will eventually become uninhabitable, then our sun will die. All these things will come to pass but do we all want to know what could be waiting for us. Would I be strong enough?

At a church service, a young lady stood up and asked abruptly and a little aggressively, if she was going to have a baby? To which the

Medium answered after a pause that she would, then brought the demonstration to an abrupt end. I asked after the service why she closed so quickly, and the reason given was. The answer yes was correct, but would the baby be happy and healthy? Likewise, my three predictions fall short, will I have a painless death and how much time does humanity have before the earth becomes uninhabitable?

During a service, a message was given and could be verified, including information regarding a new car, but there was one resounding no, the Medium had said the car was going to be red. The recipient, a young man, couldn't stand red cars, but some weeks later he met with the Medium and informed her that in collecting his blue car, the colour was red, as the wrong colour was put on the paperwork. Sounds like an amazing prediction, but Spirit was already aware of the error when the message was given.

The consequences of the recipient misinterpreting the message are high, so I am always careful how I deliver that information, even to the point of deciding not to give it at all. The responsibility and consequences rest totally with me. From the rostrum, I was telling a young man not to keep letting go of the steering wheel, as I was being shown his habit of continually taking his hands off. I had the impression of a near miss or collision, so I asked if this was a habit of his, and he confirmed it was. So, I advised he should always stay in complete control and explained what I was being shown. About three weeks later I went back to the same church and was thanked immediately by the young man as not long after I'd given the message he was nearly involved in a collision, sure if he had been driving in his usual manner things could have turned out very differently.

There are those who say I should pass on all spirit give me, but the responsibility is mine. Therefore, I do sometimes think before opening my mouth.

There would be a lot of wealthy Medium's if you could predict the lottery numbers, and yes, I have tried, and yes, I was disappointed. Why won't it work? I believe only probable outcomes can be shown, and the lottery numbers are totally random. I purchased a crystal ball and went through the long exercise of purification. Now I've given it away for I had no wish to use it.

I am a consciousness receiving information from a nonphysical entity, yet I trust what I'm shown. Although, it wasn't always that way.

When I first started, I received symbolic images. If I was shown a Wheelbarrow, it symbolised someone was carrying guilt and needed to tip it out. A spinning top represented spinning out of control usually with reference to a child. However, things changed when I had a spinning top made of tin that had seen better days and played a simple tune, and as I described it, the lady explained it was the top she had just bought. But back to the subject of prediction. I trust and in doing so am sometimes astounded. Interpretation of fleeting impressions may be enough to provide evidence of survival after physical death but to tell what the future holds tends to place Mediumship at the end of the pier as entertainment, cross my palm with silver and all that. There is a place for that still, and may well be a starting point for some, but mediumship deals with specifics, who, what, where and when. All information relates to the now or the past or the near future.

THE DOOR TO HAPPINESS

This is an important door and for many the most difficult to open. I am lucky, but things didn't always go as they should. I plan ahead, and keeping workforce and customers happy can be tricky, but I enjoy what I do as a day job, but that wasn't always the case. Not until I opened myself to the unseen world. As with all of us problems crop up, and we react. We run over all decisions, what will happen if this or that happens. We run over the scenarios visualising the probable outcomes, more than likely running over the negative ones more than the positive. It wasn't till I delved into my linking to the spirit world and came to realise Mind, Body and Spirit has a vital part to play in our happiness, health and overall wellbeing. Thinking of all the possible outcomes draws the attention to what could go wrong, and in doing so, I experience all the negative aspects of that outcome. As I rested my head on the pillow and before sleep took me I would run through the events of the day, and in doing that envisaged all the negative outcomes. Then I would start thinking about the future till sleep took me. My career path in design, engineering and art took me to be a designer, design and development manager, then to a Marketing Director. Now you would think that would be okay, but with those jobs came responsibility and stress. Don't get me wrong I still enjoyed the day job, but not as I do now. The second part of this book focuses on the Mind, Body and Spirit element in a little more detail, but for now, let say that regardless of how you feel, it is possible for you to experience true happiness. My understanding of this has only come about from the process of opening myself to Spirit, for in doing so I centre myself in the present because thinking of future problems will result in bring those problems into existence, but to promote happiness you need to think of the positive things, or best still live in the moment. You need to centre yourself as I do when I open myself to work as a Medium. I'm centred. I am in the moment. I am paying attention to the emotions and feelings of that time. The practice of connecting to another world has helped me in my daily life, and I've become happier, calmer and more understanding.

When I have a connection, I am the observer. I do not emotionally connect although I have empathy, as I've said I hear voices, suffer mood swings, have images play over in my mind, plus touch, smell, pain and the feeling my body is not my own, but I'm standing back. Analysing would make the process fail as I need to be in a place between thought. Intuition, that voice from within tells me these are not my thoughts and feelings, and I observe. This is where the magic for me happens.

I focus on the present; it's only now that exists. I can't do anything about the past, and the future is dependent on my actions. I don't dwell on mistakes if only this and what if that, will only draw my attention away from now. If I've made a mistake, I acknowledge it and accept I am human and place it behind me. (A person who has never made a mistake has never done anything.) It's an old saying, but true. Hobbies you feel passionate about where you need to focus, promote happiness because you are concentrating and past and future seem to melt away. Try to give yourself time each day to sit calmly and don't try to think of anything just be aware of your breath. When thoughts come to your mind don't push them back acknowledge them, and let them pass, don't dwell on them. Try to give yourself ten minutes each day; you will find that this will help promote awareness of the present. If I had money, fame and fortune would I be the happiest person on the planet?

Then I think of George Michael, Peter Sellers and Tony Hancock! Fame and fortune have failed many and having everything money can buy is not the key, but living in the present, and forgiving yourself for all your past errors is. You are not the person you were the other day, all the cells except for a few in your brain have regenerated. Not only is your body not the same but also you've added experiences that have helped you grow and develop. Change happens, your ego may not like it, but change is a constant. So forgive yourself and stay connected to the NOW. More on the Mind, Body and Spirit Later.

THE DOOR THAT BYPASSES THE EGO

I am connected to every living thing, and my true self is uncomplicated and is content. I'm never isolated or separated from what surrounds me. Some people will go through their lives never knowing their true self, as their ego takes hold. My true self is the source of my happiness, but my ego or human condition will always oppose my higher self. I do not deny my ego but accept it as a requirement of the human condition. I am both the light and the dark, capable of good or evil, for I am human. The key to the door that bypasses the ego is within everyone's grasp, but the ego will do all in its power to keep it hidden, so you must look for it. The story of Adam and Eve living in complete contentment in the Garden of Eden, until the time when their perception changed is more than just a story. A friend of mine visited a small village in the Gambia where their toilets were no more than holes in the ground, and they cooked over open fires. Their simple lifestyle would be considered poor in the west, but she spoke of their happy nature and described how they were constantly smiling and laughing. So who is the poorer, the worried millionaire or the villagers my friend visited? Developing this skill has helped me see that living in this world with its misguided preconceptions hold no real power over me. Yes, I hold on to hopes and dreams the same as everyone else, but I understand I am able to influence my state of mind, and every good and bad lesson from my past has helped create the person I am today, and my ego is a necessary element in that. Some see mediumship as a way of making money, but others like me are lucky enough to see its real value. You hold the key as I do, we are no different, just take a close look at yourself, and if you look hard enough, you will see things that you have never seen before. The stress you create, yes it's you that creates it, no one else. Others may try to pressurise you but it's you who gets fretful, thoughts and images are created by your mind. This is the basis of the stress. If you understand this principle, you can improve your life and move to a new level.

My ego is a necessary evil for without it, I wouldn't be able to survive, but I see it for what it is. When I was born, I had no knowledge of self; I experienced through touch, smell, taste and I could only make out blurry shapes. First being aware of my body then my mother, because when I needed sustenance, there it was. I was lucky and given love and care; I felt I had some importance, that's how my ego was conceived, then I started to forget my true self, and over time my ego became more complex, but the real me, the spirit me, is not concerned with my ego and its games. The real me is uncomplicated and prepared to wait. Our egos are part of being human, and the key to the door for further understanding is in recognising that fact. If you unlock the door, stand back and observe you can see the ego for what it is.

THE DOOR TO THE BRAIN

The brain is an electrochemical organism estimated to have billions of interconnected nerve cells. Electrical activity coming from the brain can be shown in the form of brain waves, and there are four main types. Beta waves 15 to 40 cycles per second. Beta waves are in use during periods of activity when the brain is aroused, such as during conversation. The next frequency is Alpha. This has 9 to 14 cycles per second. We are in an alpha state after completing a task, or when we are in a reflective state. If you went for a walk in the countryside, you would probably be in an Alpha state.

Theta is the next frequency and ranges between 5 and 8 cycles a second. When we begin to daydream, we are often in this state, and this is when we are prone to a flow of ideas. Finally, we have the Delta state this is when the brain waves are of the greatest amplitude and the slowest frequency around a range of 1.5 to 4 cycles per second. When we are in a deep dreamless sleep, this would take us down to the lowest frequency, typically, 2 to 3 cycles a second.

If it went down to zero, you would be considered brain dead.

The same brain wave states are common in men, women and children.

When you are in an aroused state and operating in beta, there still exist traces of the other three states.

We dream in 90-minute cycles. Active dreaming takes place during periods of rapid eye movement called REM sleep.

The relationship between consciousness and the brain is an enigma. Neurologists believe that the mind is located in the brain and that consciousness is the result of the electrochemical neurological activity. However, there is no research yet that conclusively shows that the higher levels of mind such as intuition, insight, creativity, imagination, understanding, thought, reasoning, intent, decision, knowing, will, spirit, or soul is located in brain tissue. It has been found that the mind continues to work when brain activity has been reduced under anaesthesia. It has been shown while brain waves were nearly absent; the mind was just as active, as in the waking state. Also, researchers have reported awareness in comatose patients. There is also evidence that shows reduced cortical arousal can still maintain conscious awareness.

Is it possible that whilst I work as a medium the trace elements are brought into play to achieve the physical connection to allow communication from Spirit?

All that is mentioned above applies to the connection to our physical body. I believe that when we cross over, we exist totally outside of the physical and material constraints with no loss of our personality. So, if we are cantankerous and a pain in the bum whilst in the physical, we will still be a pain in the bum on the other side. In other words, I prefer to believe that consciousness is connected to spirit and the brain is connected to the body. However, this all gets put into perspective when I receive validation on a message from the spirit world, as the how and why then seem irrelevant.

THE DOOR OF UNDERSTANDING

I stand back and view life as an observer, rather than reacting to situations. When I connect to a spirit, a flood of feelings and emotions pour out. To remain calm and connected I have to understand these are not my feelings, therefore being nonjudgmental and having empathy without taking onboard all the emotional turmoil is vital, that's if I want to remain sane.

It's all well and good for someone who has been born in the affluent West to tell someone that they have chosen the life they lead when a large proportion of the world's population lives in fear and poverty. Children are dying due to a lack of water or food. Genocide, terrorism and oppression continue around the world. Why does God let this happen? A question I have heard all too often, but the truth is we are the ones responsible for this world, it's been left in our charge, and through action or inaction, we have all made our mark. Would God be so cruel to let a child die in agony through a lack of basic food? Society, governments, multinationals, dictatorships and religious organisations, try to keep a balance and hold things together but sometimes they get it wrong, but they try. Our moral code is formed from our experiences and teaching, and if the social order has done its job, our moral code will be in line with the society we live in. If you go to war and you kill, it's considered just, but if you kill outside the law of that society, you will be classed as a murderer. (During the First World War the fighting stopped one Christmas, and both sides played a game of makeshift football. It took no time for them to realise that those they were trying to kill were no different, and even worshipped the same God. My Grandfather was one of those men. The officers tried to regain control to resume the fighting, but as my father told me, from that moment on, they shot over the heads of the perceived enemy. We are all influenced and controlled to some degree by those who have authority. It's the job of the schools and universities to condition us, to make us productive citizen. They're not interested in the spiritual you but in the corporal you. Giving you the tools for living in an ever more demanding world. To survive now, you need different skills to those in the seventeenth century and life will be unrecognisable in another two thousand years and what skills will you need then? The great spiritual teachers of the past have been misquoted and misrepresented. Jesus, Mohamed, (Blessings be upon him,) Buddha and others have tried to influence people, but many have died at the hands of extremists who've taken it upon themselves to exert authority and force views of one teaching as opposed to another.

The population at the time of Jesus was around 300 million and now stands at over seven billion, and it doesn't take a genius or prophet to see what could lie ahead, but as the world turns and time advances things change. What was okay two hundred years ago isn't acceptable today, and likewise what is okay today will sometime in the future be considered unacceptable.

You are one individual, but if you can stand back as an observer, you will see things as they really are. You will recognise the ego's fear and its eagerness to control. As an observer, it may sometimes seem that your quiet voice of reason is lost in the crowd of fearful cries, but the person standing next to you may just hear. You cannot heal the world, but you can make a difference.

Show kindness and unconditional love, and you will see it repaid tenfold.

You are a Spiritual being not just sinew and bone, you are much more than that, and it's only you who can unlock this door and step over the threshold.

THE DOOR TO HELL

All Mediums get glimpses into that other place, although its true nature is beyond our full understanding, each time we open ourselves we get a feeling of what it may be like. From what I've been shown I'm convinced that Hell as an actual place doesn't exist. However, some create their own hell, either in this world or in the next. Working as a rescue Medium has made me realise that we are quite capable of creating our own hell like the individual from the First World War who thought himself wounded in no-mans-land. The world he'd created was quite alarming, so Hell can exist, but not as a place but as a state created by fear and anger. Established religious teaching gives backing to the concept of Hell. The Koran (Quran) depicts hell as a place of raging fire. Like the Christian belief and in Hinduism, there is also a similar realm, but I'd like you to consider that light and dark are two sides of the same coin, just as the male and female elements, the yin and yang. In the material world, Hell exists for some, because genocide, mass murder and rape take place all too often. I don't know what happens to those who have committed such atrocities once they pass from this world, but from what I have been shown I believe the perpetrators are treated with understanding and helped till full realisation of what they did and the effect it had on others. I don't feel they are judged other than through their own realisation. I think that they are not persecuted or punished but are shown the consequences of their actions. We are not equipped to comprehend how the other dimensions function, but I constantly hear the passage from the Bible. 'In my Father's house are many mansions.'

The Church I'm sure used the threat of Hell and damnation as a way of controlling. However, consider people who are mentally unstable and have a personality disorder that manifests in extreme antisocial behaviour, they are still spiritual entities. They are not sane, due to their malfunctioning and acting in a way that most consider abnormal. However, when they pass from this world to the next, they are no longer restricted by their physical limitations. They are shown the results of their actions and helped to full understanding. I've fallen short and done things I'm not proud of in this life, but would God be so cruel to condemn me to burn in the fires of Hell for eternity? Would it not be wiser to cure me and help me to make recompense?

THE DOOR TO HEAVEN

St Peter waits at the gate with a list as long as your arm. Will we be allowed in? Do we get issued with a harp and white robe? Yet another section from the Bible resonates. 'Behold the kingdom of heaven is at hand' or 'the kingdom of God is within you.' You are Spirit, and no harm can come to the real you, the Spirit you. I've been so lucky throughout my life that my world's not far from being heavenly, okay it could be better sometimes, but I for one am not complaining. As long as you can understand your true essence and recognise the ego for what it is and not let it control your every move, you will create your own heaven here on Earth.

When I pass from this life to the next, I will be free from the constraints of the Material dimension and the laws that apply to it; they will no longer be relevant. My thoughts can draw me to the future, and take me away from the present, leading me to question what if this and what if that, and when this happens it will lead me away from happiness. Heaven can be reached here and now, and It takes no effort. I will go into this in a little more depth in the Mind, Body and Spirit section, but when I get out of bed on a cold morning and travel to work, I don't think of what the day will bring, I concentrate on what I am doing at that very moment, I feel the crispness in the air and think how refreshing it is. I drive to work and marvel at the technology that gets me to my destination. I try to pay attention to all the little things that make that moment so special. Heaven is at our fingertips and within our grasp, if we would only be aware of what is happening this very second.

GOD or GOD'S DOOR

You may say divine mind, Singularity, Divine spirit, God, Universal consciousness or higher self. A word is just a word, but in writing this section, I need to tread carefully and first say that what you believe is fine, I would never be so arrogant as to question anyone's concept of the divine. Some tend to get defensive about their faith, but I am not questioning that either, but for me, faith is not on the table because although working as a Medium sometimes makes me question my sanity, and if it wasn't for positive validation, I would have checked myself into a psychiatric unit years ago. However, having had a connection to the unseen world has made me see life through different eyes. Maybe I am deluded and should have been committed, but I would like to place my theory in front of you. Even if you see God as a wise old man sitting on a throne somewhere in the heavens or consider God as an all perceiving consciousness, consider this. We exist and are constructed of atoms, and our spirit-self uses this body whilst also connected to the divine, God or as I sometimes say the singularity. Therefore we all have a thread of connection to the divine, and that connection remains even when we discard our physical bodies. It is impossible for me to understand or comprehend God, but I am sure the connection that I have or to be more precise we all have, is in some way part of a more complex picture.

THE DOOR TO THE LIBRARY

Throughout the ages, we have tried to record events. Storage and the retention of information has always been considered significant, but by placing that information in the public domain, it is liable to take on a life of its own. Someone else will use it, and the information could be misused or distorted. We all add to the storehouse of information, either directly or indirectly but once it's out there, no one can stop what happens to it. It may get distorted through misunderstanding or intentionally. Trying to find anything historical, trawling through the vast amount of documented evidence can be a bit of a test. How much is accurate? Two accounts of the same event can be so different depending on the preconceptions and position of the observer. False memory will also come into play. Even if you carefully record the information it could get lost, then you are left with interpretations and assumptions rather like the writings of Confucius. The world will change, and the accumulation of knowledge is fundamental to scientific and spiritual development. Information takes on a life of its own once handed over. Would Leonardo Da Vinci have produced better work if he had the latest PC and software and how would Blaise Pascal have done with the tools that now lie at our disposal? Hopefully, advances can be made that will make this world a better place. Now we can all add to the storehouse of information thanks to the continued development of technology. A few years ago I had a tape of my daughters with giggles and laughter, but the tape itself has long since been lost, and I don't own a tape player now. Nothing ever stays the same and things will constantly change. I can say I have had information validated that has not been gained through normal physical senses, and one day I hope that science will take a closer look at mediumship. I am fascinated with the struggle between spiritual knowledge and science and how some get worked up about thoughts and views opposed to their own. I am open to views opposed to mine as it makes me question. I understand that for some, it may be a little disconcerting, having fundamental principles questioned, but for me standing still isn't an option.

THE LETTERBOX

As soon as the letter hits the mat, there is no going back. It's posted, and no amount of banging on the door will stop it from being seen. Once opened the information it holds can't be erased. You will consider what I've written and may discard it as the ramblings of a madman, but I can't erase your memory or turn the clock back. yet let me tell you this, nothing is as straightforward as it first seems. We will have differing opinions and views and what works for one won't work for another, but I've been lucky to have had gained insight into another world a world we will all experience one day. The connection I have to the unseen world can be compared to shouting and looking through a letterbox. The view is restricted, and I can only see areas of the hall not into the living room and trying to communicate with someone when you can't see them can be tricky. However, just because it's a little difficult doesn't mean I shouldn't give it a go. You will have your own views on the continuation of the personality after physical death and no doubt you have heard of others experiences. There is no need to dedicate your life to becoming a Medium unless you wish to, but please believe me when I say that in connecting and gaining validation removes any doubt as to the existence of this other world, regardless of the name you wish to give it. I hope the information I put before you enables you to build a solid foundation for you to grow, but if you think I'm deluded, I wouldn't be offended, because regardless of what you or I believe the end result will be the same.

THE SIDE DOOR

I am fascinated with the struggle between science and spiritual knowledge, but I'm convinced that one-day ample resources will be found to fund research into life after physical death. Ample funding has been made available for other aspects of the physical world, and this important element should not be left totally in the hands of people like me. Some get worked up when views opposed to their own are voiced, yet all anyone wants is the truth or at least taking tiny steps towards it. Okay, it can be disconcerting, having your fundamental principles being questioned and Mediums are not exempt from this. Most think Mediums a bit odd, and what we do trivial, so I'm not surprised that science hasn't looked at this subject as it should. Mediumship is presented through the many spiritualist organisations, where we stand in front of a congregation and provide evidence of a continuation of the personality after physical death. I do feel through mediumship a larger truth can be found. The world is awash with psychics and Mediums some making a good living out of their skill. The English Government has changed the 1951 fraudulent Mediums Act in favour of a EU directive that will leave many Mediums open to prosecution. (*Well, at least, I won't be burnt at the stake.*) It's important to provide evidence that substantiates the theory that death is an illusion, thereby helping in some way to remove the fear of death. Stage Mediumship helps in that process as well, but Mediums are only people. Why do I do it, I've asked myself that many times, but when I have a connection it feels right. Okay so giving messages from uncle Joe who passed away twenty years ago is important to the recipient, but there is more to the process than that. As historians try to unravel mysteries of the past and scientists prove or disprove theories, Mediums should be working to provide evidence of life after death, but as practitioners, we are not taken seriously. We all contribute to the storehouse of knowledge. There are some who devote their lives to help whilst others only want to satisfy their own needs, yet each contributes to this time. I only have a limited period left to walk on this earth, and you may think being a Medium gives me the answers, but it does exactly the opposite. It does, however, remove the fear of death, but also opens a box that contains many more questions. The universe is a bloody big place, full of stuff. Billions of stars and many of those will have planets like our earth. but never think what you do as minor, or of little value, for you are playing your part. You and I are not insignificant, it may seem like it when you look up at the stars and contemplate the enormity of it all, but you have a duty to yourself to live your life free of fear and enjoy every moment.

THE DOOR TO DREAMS

A good nights sleep is needed to maintain a healthy body, but the amount is not written in stone. We all have different sleep patterns, and our internal clock controls the neurotransmitter, and my internal clock may run faster than yours, but let's not get bogged down with the how or why. Some people require more sleep than others. Winston Churchill and Margret Thatcher were reported to function on very little sleep without loss of energy. As stated earlier, we dream in 90-minute cycles. When delta frequencies increase into theta, and active dreaming takes place during periods of rapid eye movement or REM sleep. Studies are still being undertaken into the science of sleep because little is known about this nightly occurrence. The subconscious is very powerful, and dreams could be a way of helping us survive. The Australian Aboriginal people have a belief in a spiritual other world called Dreamtime. Psychoanalyst Sigmund Freud's book 'Die Traumdeutung' is a reference work on the theory of the unconscious connection to dreaming, but I would like to place another theory before you, that is, during sleep Spirit entities can interact, imparting visions and feelings in the mind of the person dreaming. During sleep, the body rests and what happens to the Spirit or subconscious is at this stage conjecture, but I've known people who have had attached entities that have played havoc with their sleep pattern. One young lady was grateful that at last, she could talk to someone about her situation, without them thinking her insane. Explaining how orbs and spiritual forms came to her just before sleep. She never felt threatened, but drained, and getting a good night's sleep was near impossible. As soon as her head hit the pillow the visions started, none were particularly pleasant. Different people would come and go, and this had become a regular occurrence. I explained that sensitive people could pick up memories and feelings from a single spiritual entity or many. Thinking her house haunted a local spiritualist church was asked to help, and they acknowledged a spirit was there, but they were unable to do anything, saying the entity was uncooperative and just wouldn't go, hence her attendance on a wet and windy Friday night at our open Circle to get some guidance and find out what was happening. Almost straight away one of the men in the group could hear a young girl laughing. He described a small hill and open fields. Maybe a little explanation is needed. Remember whatever is visualised will influence the Spirit's perception and vice versa. Visualisation is a key; it's like daydreaming, so when the man thought he could hear the young girl, it was as if he was reading a story and seeing it in his mind's eye. Now let's get back to the Circle. As soon as the relaxation meditation had finished, a number of people had a feeling of discomfort and the impression of disorientation. The young lady who had the problem said she could make out the form of an old lady bent and twisted standing between the two people sitting opposite. I could tell that the connection was strong, so I lost no time, working as quickly as I could. I explained to the apparition of the old lady she could stop the pain because she no longer had a physical body, but the old lady was trapped in her own world. I offered a folded plain white dress explaining it was magic and if worn, she would look and feel younger. We tried hard to lift her mood, but it had no effect. So I tried another tack, and asked if there was one thing she could have, what would it be? After a pause, told us of a man who we assumed to be her husband. Then a number of us sense the presence of a dog running around being a nuisance, and as soon as one of the Circle mentioned it, she said, 'It's me dog'.

Then without another word turned and walked away, leaving the dog running around. We needed her to come back, but the dog wouldn't wander far from his mistress, so we knew the old lady hadn't gone far. We visualised a small table with a chair similar to any you'd find in a back-street pub and on it placed a bottle and glass. We knew we had caught her interest but now she stood just outside the Circle, but it wasn't enough to entice her back in. The connection hadn't been broken and now wasn't the time to back off. Knowing that she wanted her man we asked if he could come forward, and we didn't have to wait long. Saying he was a gentleman would have been stretching a point. He immediately sat at the table. I was disappointed because I was hoping that the man she wanted could help, but I knew we now had two trapped souls. We asked if he wanted anything in particular. Then without much of a pause, he said abruptly, 'Meat and potato pie'.

So we placed a freshly baked pie on the table and laid two places, asking her to sit and join him.

'I wouldn't eat that muck, look at im!' She sneered.

The woman wasn't happy, but the dog was, it was sitting close by, looking up at his master. You know how some couples love to disagree, sniping and always wanting to have the last word. This felt just like that, no matter what we were to do, getting these two together was going to be impossible. Leaving him to his pie, we turned our attention to the twisted old lady and told her not to be concerned about him, trying to draw her attention away from the man sitting at the table. We needed to get her out of this situation, so I asked her to tell me about a time when she was really happy. It was quick we all had the same impression of rolling hills, green grass and wildflowers dotted about. We had managed to move her thoughts away, from that negative situation. So now we needed to continue in the same direction. We all created that scene in our mind's eye, just as the young man had described before the session had got fully underway. The laughter of a young girl happy in such beautiful countryside was what was needed. We placed her firmly in the middle of the picture. Now she was no longer an old lady, but a young woman, wearing the simple white dress like the one we offered before. We could see an older lady on the horizon, then as the young lady ran up the hill and across the open fields, she became even younger, running into the outstretched arms of the waiting woman. Then without looking back, they were gone. This left the dog and man to deal with. The dog was still at his side watching him devour his meat and potato pie. We tried hard to get through to him but to no avail. We knew this was going to be tricky, both dog and man caught in their own little world not comprehending what was happening. So we decided to do the best we could. I explained that we were going to place a protective field around them. First, we visualised a multicoloured force field surrounding the dog. It was happy inside this bubble of protective light. We watched as the swirling energy pulsated. Then two spirits looking like angels approached and lifted the animal lovingly and took it safely away. The man didn't take much notice, being engrossed in his pie. So we duplicated the process of creating this protective ball of energy around him also. He seemed to be calmer as we created it. I explained once more that this was being done for his protection, and not to worry. As soon as the ball of energy had surrounded him, His hard expression softened as the same two beings approached and led him happily away. It didn't take long for the Circle to return to normality. The young lady appeared to be relieved as I gave her my phone number just in case, but to-date I've heard nothing.

I've had other instances where sleep has been disturbed by a Spirit trying to interact. What they were picking up on were the feelings and memories of the attachment. I'm sure that a spirit can cause restless sleep. They can't do harm other than draining our energy, but the person affected needs to regain control. Spirit exists outside our material dimension. They may not even be aware of what they are doing. They may just feel comfortable in someone's energy, as thoughts and feelings are shared. So protection must be reinforced. Then the entity needs to be moved on, not banished, never to darken the door again, but helped. We have touched on both subjects already, but let's revisit them, taking the assumption that you are the one with the problem of an attachment.

As you prepare for sleep, ask for the highest help that Spirit can provide, then say in your head, 'I'm powerful, calm and non-judgmental.' Say it a number of times to yourself, but don't just say it; believe it, because spirit picks up on your thoughts. Don't doubt your strength as you visualise a bright light shining from your core. See it radiate out, know this is the light of divine protection. The spirit will see you as a glowing powerful non-threatening entity. In addition, they must perceive you as being non-judgmental and full of love. Then relax and demand space by asking them to stand back so you can get adequate rest. Be strong in your commitment you will be surprised at the results. Transcended spirits will never be a cause for concern, as they will always be sympathetic and loving, but trapped entities can make it seem as if the person with the attachment has psychological problems. Sleep is needed to keep the body functioning, but the Spirit never sleeps.

The phenomenon of astral travel takes place when the body is at rest. The sensations felt when the Spirit parts from the body is a rushing sound, together with a twisting sensation. A cord with infinite elasticity joins the spirit to the body. When in this state you can travel at the speed of thought and to anywhere in the known cosmos. I have experienced it once where I stood at the foot of our bed, but as I looked at where I lay, in a flash, I found myself back in my body. The experience was not unpleasant, but I am unsure whether it was a lucid dream or an actual astral experience. I've had many spiritual encounters and know how powerful the mind can be so to say I've experienced Astral travel would be incorrect, although all the factors seemed to be there.

I believe time and space are only relevant to the material dimension, and the spirit world is not held to the laws of the material but follow different restrictions. The rules that govern the spirit world are unknown to us, and in our present material state mainly irrelevant. Would you want a child to grow up too quickly missing the wonders and mystery that childhood brings? The same could be said about trying to understand something out of our grasp, so don't waste too much time contemplating them, as the present is where attention needs to be focused.

Lucid dreaming is where the person sleeping is aware and able to control what is happening within the dream. The brain is a wonderful processing system and sleep could be a way for the subconscious to work through issues. I would like to think that sleeping allows our higher selves to communicate and interact. Every time we dream, we are opening a door into a world where the impossible is experienced. So keeping a notebook by the bed isn't a bad idea. Answers and solutions to problems have often been found through dreams. There are many documented examples where dreams have helped in the creation of art and literature as well as other creative avenues. Surrealism was born out of dreams, and Mary Shelley's nightmare was penned into Frankenstein. How many times have you said, 'Let's sleep on it'? A problem occurs that you need a solution for and low and behold after a good restful night the answer is found. The mind is very powerful and although the brain has been mapped much is still to be understood. Hypnosis is an induced psychological state and has been used effectively for years in clinical procedures, although stage hypnosis shows this practice in a somewhat poor light, it has been demonstrated to have beneficial effects on pain reduction and the promotion of healing.

THE DOOR TO PAST LIVES.

Many say that you and I have existed forever and were neither created nor made. We are part of the breath of God. Although I've communicated with the spirit world, I've no feeling as to its truth, yet I have spoken to many who believe they have walked on the earth before. A few have gone through past life regression. through hypnosis, some have relived elements of what they assume to be their past life's. if our spirit self already knows this, do we need to relive what could be traumatic and unconnected to our present condition? I may discover that I was a mass murderer or that I did horrific things or had them done to me. Past lives are that, past, and hold little relevance to this point in time, but regardless of my personal views, several people have gained something from the experience. Studies have been undertaken where some remember who they were prior to the life they live now, without any assistance from past life regression therapy. Cases have been studied that show some compelling evidence, such as the case of James Larsen who recounted stories of his life as a World War II pilot, shot down by the Japanese. All this information is easy to research as it's well documented. The thing that I find interesting from a number of these cases is that the information was obtained during sleep. Little two-year-old James was found in his bed screaming. 'Plane on Fire.' Then from there, the story unfolds. The information imparted in most cases is impressive, although the sceptics would say it was coincidence or fraud. I would ask you to consider another possibility, could it be a Spirit connection and not actually his past life? Delving into subjects like this only raises more questions, but you and I exist now, in this life. I have no doubt you have watched Paul McKenna working to rid someone of a phobia using hypnosis, and it's now used sometimes in dentistry and minor surgery. The biomechanical processing unit we use to function is fragile, and for some hypnosis has helped them cope.

listening to the radio I realised, most of the artists were no longer with us. Okay, three score years and ten may no longer apply in 2019, but life on earth still has its conclusion. This world isn't an illusion. It's very real yet fleeting. Time in this existence is limited. If we could stand back and look at the world from the perspective of Spirit what would we see? Maybe this insane world has never been any different with those in positions of power making sure they could hold on to it, and those holding vast wealth trying to make even more. The world is a mixed-up place with some extreme violence and cruelty counterbalanced by some amazing kindness. The time you and I have been given is ours to do with as we wish. You may think you have little influence in the world, but that's not true for even doing nothing affects those around us, just as much as taking action. We are time travellers and exist this very second, then moving on to the next. Your journey starts with your first step like a pebble dropped into still water the ripples travel further than you think. Before we walk through the door with the large red exit sign above, take stock. Think of all the amazing things you've done and all the incredible experiences you've had. Take time out every day to be grateful, for the things in your life. Even when you are in poor health, remember this life is for a living. Do not waste a single second of it. Mediumship is an amazing part of my life and has opened the door to a deeper understanding. Mediumistic ability isn't just about giving messages; It's much more than that. As we close the door behind us on this first section, I thank you for walking with me. Always listen to that small voice within and let it guide you as you journey through the maze of life.

SECTION TWO
The Mind, Body and Spirit Connection

INTRODUCTION TO PART TWO

Opening myself to the unseen world has made me delve deeper into the Mind, Body, Spirit connection, and like my phone, I'm continually updating, I first created these elements for the Open Circle. However, this platform seems a good way to get the information in front of others. I will explain how the connection between Mind, Body and Spirit has helped me. You may notice the similarity between both sections of this book, but it's intentional. We are human and have different ideas and views, so please read the following with an open mind allowing time between each element so you can give careful consideration to what has been written.

BODY MIND SPIRIT

Basic Understanding of Your True Nature. (Very basic.)

If you go into a bookshop, you would probably find this book in the MIND BODY SPIRIT section, and that's not a bad place to start as your conscious and subconscious, have an impact on your body, and your body is what your spirit or superconscious use to experience this existence. Well, I did say this is the basic understanding. The three elements of mind, body and spirit are connected and function as a cohesive unit.

The body you have is yours to use for as long as you live, it is a biomechanical unit where nutrients go in, and waste comes out. We are conceived, born and live as best we can, finally the body fails and perishes. Each of us is unique. We have different sexual preferences, physical abilities and beliefs. You may think your uniqueness makes you separate or stand-alone, but this is far from the truth.

Open a newspaper, listen to the news, turn on the television, and you are bombarded with information, most of it negative. Put aside the spiritual aspect of our connection for a moment, and see the simple fact that it is impossible to exist physically isolated from the world. Your body functions on this planet and is reliant on the earth's vegetation to supply oxygen and substance. I live in England, so when I turn the tap on water flows, therefore I am reliant on those who work to keep the water system functioning, and I expect the light to turn on when I flick the switch. The planet's population is growing fast, and as a species, we need to work together if we want to survive. Even if you were totally isolated your body would never survive without water, and for the continuation of the species, you need to find a mate. In the world of today, we are bombarded with information where natural and manmade disasters are described in graphic detail. Only the other day a news report was about how our health service is failing, social services underfunded, and the fabric of our society is falling apart, but the United Kingdom's National health service didn't exist prior to July 5th, 1948 and Charles Dickens made a good income from writing about the poor social conditions of his time. Today you can have surgery undertaken pain-free. Illnesses like Polio and Rickets have all but been eradicated. Okay, it's not a perfect world, and it will either get better or worse because change is the only constant. Wars will be waged, and people will continue to do stupid things. We live in a world full of uncertainties. However, you are more than a biomechanical entity; you have aspirations, want to be healthy and loved. So let's take a closer look. Your brain, that grey stuff between your ears processes approximately ten quadrillion calculations a second. Wow, you are a supercomputer. Every thought, action voluntary and involuntary is handled by your supercomputer the brain. The impulse sent to the mussels of your heart and breathing is done without you having to think. About seventy billion of your cells are renewed every day, so your body is in a constant state of renewal and if you want to function effectively requires looking after. However, there is another element that I will call, for now, the conscious self. Any name you wish to give it is an inaccuracy as science as yet has no agreed definition for the mind. We know thinking has an impact on the body. We have busy lives, and for some, it seems there are not enough hours in the day, and day to day living is stressful. If that's you take note. Modern life can reap havoc, as continual stress brings ill health. If you are stressed your immune system is vulnerable because your metabolism will have directed all its resources to fight or flight mode, not rest and repair. Thinking can be either bad or good for your health.

MIND OR THOUGHT

A lady working in a charity shop told my wife she was leaving because working there was too stressful. So this retired lady who is willing to give her time freely feels stressed. She is not reliant on the work to provide income, so why or who is making her stressed? There is only one person responsible, have you figured it out. I work for a Harvard educated businessman, who does not suffer fools gladly. I have worked to extremely tight schedules in the past, and it was sometimes stressful. However, it was me creating that stress, no one else, just me. There are situations where stress is unavoidable, such as being trapped between two warring factions, where you or your family are likely to be shot or blown apart, but a typical work situation is different. Worrying about being fired or humiliated is not quite the same as a threat to life or limb, yet even in extream cases, stress, worry and fear come from your thoughts. Thoughts can help or hinder, and thoughts have a knack of replaying over and over again in your mind, what if this happens, what if I get it wrong, imagining all the possible outcomes, rarely positive. This is where it helps to understand negative thinking creates stress, and stress diverts energy from your immune system, and this can cause physical illness. You and I are continually thinking unless we have Mastered Zen meditation, Your thoughts have moulded you into who you are. Your mind chatters on and on, try to stop thinking for a few seconds it's impossible. If you practice meditation, you can draw your attention to a single image or repeat a mantra, but even then you end up thinking of the sound or image. Let's face it thinking is a part of life. You can control your thoughts, so try to be positive rather than negative. I presume you know of the film and publication called the Secret, (*a book by Rhonda Byrne, about the law of attraction that claims thoughts can change the world directly. Worth a read.*) then there is Bob Proctor and Louise Lynn Hay who will take you into the world of positive affirmations in more detail, but as an example, if you say, I don't think this will work, the likelihood is it won't, as you have set the seed of doubt. Instead, say, this will work, and the mind is set for a positive outcome.

You can't stop the endless chatter in your head, but you can control and direct it. Although, it's not as simple as saying our reality is created by our thinking. In no way could you say a baby dying from a debilitating disease created it, but for now, let's take a simple stance and assume thoughts can affect our perceived reality and physical wellbeing. Watching films and dramas immerse us in the experience being acted, be it good or bad and your body will react because of the emotion. Read a book, and you visualise the characters and once again live it in your mind. Thinking can be fun as well as instigating action, and action brings results, but the endless chatter in our skulls can be a distraction. Replaying what happened in the past and worrying about the future only pulls us away from the present. What has been done is done, and the future is yet to be, but what we think now and do now creates our future. The conscious and subconscious part of you is, where the ego resides. It's continuously aware of itself, whereas the Spirit you is just happy to exist and experience. The Spirit you goes by many names, but the truth is it doesn't matter what name you call it, as it recognises no name, yet all names. You've heard the expressions, gut feeling, Intuition or gut instinct. These are ways for your spirit-self to communicate with your physical self. Your gut or intuition isn't your Spirit self but the mechanism for transmitting information. Science has shown that we have dual conscious elements one for the right hemisphere and one for the left, but I believe it is a little more complex than that. I am not a scientist, but from my personal experience as a Medium, I think our personality is constructed of four major elements, the subconscious, conscious, ego and spirit self and all of these have contributed to construct the personality, and it is the personality that dictates our thoughts. When I awake I don't jump straight out of bed, I lay there for a few seconds and think to myself, this is going to be a fantastic day and smile. Carol and I always say how lucky we are, even though we are human and thereby flawed.

THE NATURE OF SPIRIT

Our physical-self is unable to completely comprehend our true spiritual nature as our ego is doing its job by helping us survive. By developing the inherent mediumistic ability Mediums are privileged to gain insight into our true nature. Some would ask you to consider that you existed prior to your birth in a nonphysical form as a spirit entity who wished to take part in the game of life. You existed before your birth and will continue to be after your physical death. I would not be so bold as to say that, but I have experienced many connections to a personality that once had a physical presence on this planet. Therefore, through personal experience, I would state that the personality continues after physical death. The nature of spirit is beyond our complete understanding, but through the connection to the unseen world, I have been privileged to get a feeling that in our spirit form we can reason and interact.

CONTINUATION OF THE PERSONALITY AFTER PHYSICAL DEATH

Although proving something to satisfy the scientific community seems an impossibility, it should not stop us from attempting the task. It is now 2018, I was conceived, born and my body will perish one day, but I have a theory that the personality continues after physical death. Others will say this is no more than wishful thinking. I can not prove my theory, but neither can the sceptic disprove it, but it makes little difference what the doubter or I think for we will all eventually arrive at that point. However, I know that developing this ability helps in everyday life. So I would like you to consider this: We are mind, body and spirit and all elements are connected whilst on this planet, and each aspect has equal importance. The simplistic view is the spiritual element of the Medium connects with the disembodied spirit enabling the Medium to pass information on. Spirit is communicating with Spirit one with a body and one without.

Development of this ability is more a journey of self-discovery than anything else, sometimes the direction I take leads to a dead end, or U-turn, but in trying to guide others, I often find they show me more. Even those who lead can sometimes get lost along the way and being a Medium doesn't give you a golden ticket or make you better than anyone else; in fact, it tends to let you see the true nature of life and how we are all connected. Most of the world's population are preoccupied with life on a physical level, so the mind and spirit element get little attention, but those who choose to take this path can gain an understanding and see the game of life as it is.

SPIRIT CONNECTING WITH SPIRIT

When the Medium brings the mind body and spirit into line and connects to the unseen world the information can be picked up in many ways. Science considers we perceive through sensory input, sight, hearing, taste, smell and touch being the five primary senses. However, there are more, like the Vestibular organ senses gravitational pull, orientation and rotation. We can detect temperature through thermoreceptors. Our nervous system is complicated, and if we delve into the subject of colour, the issue gets cloudy, as this is both objective and subjective. Our perception of the material world is restricted, as we are unable to perceive Infrasound or ultrasound. The same applies to the light spectrum. Neither do we sense the subatomic particles that are continually bombarding us. We have a limited awareness of the world we inhabit, but Mediums pick up additional information that has not been gained by normal means. I believe this has been bought about by connecting to the nonphysical world. The scientific community would require convincing evidence before even considering the mediumistic ability existed, and unfortunately so far testing in controlled conditions have bee inconclusive. A statement from Dr Carroll said, "that for there to be an afterlife; consciousness would need to be entirely separated from our physical body. But instead of an ever-lasting soul consciousness appears to be composed of a series of atoms and electrons essentially."

Now I haven't scrutinised the interview fully, but I find it fascinating that science has proof of what consciousness actually is. My Father donated his body to the University of Southampton, and now that establishment has found, 30 seconds after the heart had stopped, brain activity continues up to three minutes after pronouncement of death. The scientific community requires funding to research what I consider to be the most important question humankind will ever ask. Is there life after death?

THE GAME OF LIFE

You live in the material world, a world that is dysfunctional and imperfect, it can be cruel and kind. At any time of the day or night, there will be someone putting their life on the line to perform some selfless deed, while at the same time another person will be taking part in some awful crime. But for now, forget the rest of the world, and think of yourself. Yes, be selfish. You can't change the world until you change yourself. The steward or stewardess will inform you in the pre-flight safety instruction that if the oxygen masks fall from the compartment above your head, put yours on first before assisting others. I watch very little television and try to avoid any upsetting news as I am not able to alleviate the situation. As the saying goes, "shit happens." I am sensitive and therefore actively shield myself. I sometimes watch a film, but I know its fiction which seems okay. However, to play the game of life, you need to differentiate between black and white, but to understand the difference, you must have seen black to compare it to white. or experienced pain to know pleasure. If you were to stand in a white room with light emanating from each corner and everything in it was white, you'd be lucky to see anything. You must have understood sickness to know wellness and sadness to recognize the happy times. This is the tapestry of life, but to play the game, you must first realise that everything that has happened before this moment, as you read this is in the past. That time no longer exists. If you are anything like me you have done some terrible things, I have been thoughtless, cruel, rude and sometimes just not nice. That was in the past. You cannot go back, but you can forgive yourself, and there is no saying you won't do it again, and if you do don't beat yourself up just understand you are human. Forgiving yourself is vital for bringing your spirit-self into alignment with your physical self. Forgiving others is also necessary, this is in no way condoning their actions, but just letting go, forgiving allows you to move forward.

These documented sayings are from three spiritual teachers:

"Forgive them for they do not know what they do."

"Be merciful to others, and you will receive mercy. Forgive others, and Allah will forgive you."

"Forgive others not because they deserve forgiveness, but because you deserve peace."

If you can't forgive, you are holding on to resentment and keeping the act alive. The person you won't forgive has probably forgotten about it, and by holding on to it, you are only holding on to negative thoughts that can harm you mentally and physically. Forgive others for their ignorance as you start to align yourself you will begin to see life a little differently. Forgiveness is a fundamental element in knowing how to play the game of life.

THOUGHTS CREATE

I'm sure you will understand the reason for jumping from element to element, as each one unfolds to reveal more of itself. In the process of developing the mediumistic ability, we learn how to listen and tune into our spiritual self. Okay, the process can be different for each individual, but tuning in is the one thing we all have to get the hang of. Your thoughts have created who you are, your perception of your world has been shaped by your thoughts. The simplistic formula is that thoughts lead to actions that create the outcome.

Negative thoughts = negative outcome

Positive thoughts = positive outcome

As I have already said, developing the mediumistic ability can help in day to day living and thinking leads to action and action to results. So what do you want to accomplish, improve or do? Write it down, but don't do anything. I know you have come across the saying, be careful what you wish for, because you may get it. Life is complicated, and nothing is straightforward. I've often wanted for something only to find when I have it; the need has gone. You may wish for money yet money in its self is no more than an IOU, a document acknowledging a debt, having it, in no way guarantees happiness. True happiness comes from the understanding that you are perfect and loved. Happiness is real wealth; If you could talk to George Michael, Elvis Presley or J. P. Getty, you would soon realise money is not the solution. We need money to survive in the modern age, but happiness comes from contentment and something more profound. Thinking negative thoughts can have an adverse effect physically, emotionally and spiritually. Thinking plays a fundamental part in creating our current reality, and even if you accept this as partly true, you must admit you have the power to influence your life's path. Developing the ability to connect to the unseen world has helped me in many ways. Physical health is also a vital component to your wellbeing, and I've no doubt you're aware of the placebo effect, the sugar pill that when taken has the same effect as the drug being trialled. They are healed because of their belief. Years ago my Grandmother was given a sugar pill by her doctor as she was convinced withdrawing her current medication was a bad idea.

Thinking can affect your health, so please think positive thoughts. Read or watch Louise Hay. Although this lady passed to the world of Spirit in August 2017, she is still an inspiration thanks to the power of the internet and the publishing company she founded.

Now a word of warning, and I know you are not stupid, but I must state: The internet has this ability to promote fiction as fact quicker than the speed of light. Do not take things you read as fact, always question and use your intuition, or, as I would rather say, your connection to Spirit.

THE BODIES DEMISE

Death is what many see as the futility of life, the exit point where we end up. Let me say the ego, the self that you have constructed will do all in its power to draw your attention away from the fact that no matter what you do, or achieve, there is no way of avoiding its inevitability. Most people are petrified by the idea of existing no more, although some may think terminating their existence is preferable to continuing. I can no more prove the continuation of the personality after physical death than others can prove the contrary, but the validation I have been given as a Medium has provided me with enough evidence to say death isn't the finality most think. Nothing can be proved or disproved as to what happens after our last breath, but for me, death is the change from your constructed reality to something else. What that something else is, has yet to be determined, but as a Medium, I have an inkling. Your ego will try to distract you from the inevitability, and that's not a bad thing, as once again dwelling on something you perceive as negative has an adverse effect on your wellbeing. If on the other hand, you think like me that death as no more than going through a door into another room, fear will be reduced. This is where Mediums have an advantage, for they know that death is not as most think. Fear of death is reasonable, and many religions use that fear to keep their members in order, with the notion of hell, punishment or the promise of heaven. However, your Spirit-self is undisturbed, knowing that your not just a biomechanical entity standing alone on this planet. The fear of death can cast a shadow over life, but if you shine a light, the shadow will vanish. You an I are constructed of cells and those cells are the building blocks of our current persona. (*Persona is Latin meaning the mask, or character played by an actor.*) Your spirit-self is not your persona but stands apart, not separate although most of your waking life it is out of alignment with the mind and physical self, bringing it into alignment creates understanding beyond words and bringing Mind, Body and Spirit into balance is essential to your health and wellbeing.

the You were nurtured, sent to school then sent out to survive in society. Most of your teaching has been based on survival in an aggressive world, a world plagued by war and greed. Our most popular sports are built on the desire to be top dog, by winning and beating the opposition. Many would say that is the world of today, and they would be right, but it is a world built on flawed assumptions. You cannot change the world. However, you can change the way you live in it, by playing the game of life.

So as a quick recap:

Thought has helped create your physical self.

Negative thoughts promote negative results

Positive thoughts encourage positive results

Thoughts effect Health

Death of the physical body is inevitable

Death of the soul or spirit is unproven

Being aware of your Spirit Self promotes wellbeing.

ALIGNMENT OF THE THREE ELEMENTS

I have been openly criticised for my views by those who consider they are special and have been bestowed the gift of mediumship, For I believe we are all capable of connecting to the world of spirit. Some have chosen to develop the mediumistic ability, and when the connection is made it could be considered a gift, but Mediums are not superhuman or special. The method of bringing mind, body and spirit into alignment is simple for that's your natural state, but put aside the thought of connecting to the Spirit world as for now I want you to align your spiritual self with your mind and body. I do not want you to hold your body in a physical Yoga posture, but I do want you to become aware of your physical self.

Mind - Your thoughts will wander, and the internal noise in your head will continue, let it. Pay your wandering thoughts no heed, but consider each action you undertake in the exercise of relaxation. Think through every step. Use your imagination to feel and visualise every stage.

Body - Sit and make yourself comfortable. Start by wiggling your toes and relax them, be aware of each one and all the tiny mussels that control them, feel them relax and visualise the tendons letting go. Now draw your attention to your feet and do the same. You are using your mind to visualise the action of relaxing. Feel with your senses and visualise each area relax, then slowly work your way up your body. Don't make this too drawn out; you can do this quicker than you think, but make sure you draw your attention to each area. When you get to your upper torso, you can wiggle your fingers and work your way up your arms till you reach your shoulders. Finally, work through the tendons in your neck and the numerous mussels in your face right to the tip of your head. If you have fallen asleep, don't be worried it just means your body needed rest. You have ample time, and there is no rush. This is easy to do, and if you do this exercise a few times, you will become quicker at relaxing. You may find your thoughts wander but just bring your awareness back to the task.

Spirit - Your spirit self is happy to experience and exist, and the persona, ego and physical aspects of you are like the clothes you wear to face the world. In relaxing the body, you are bringing your spirit self into balance, but we live in the real world, a world that is dysfunctional and can sometimes be difficult to face. Some will be able to undertake the relaxation exercise with ease while others will find it difficult. Being able to relax is important for mental and physical health, and may for some seem an impossible hill to climb, but repeat this exercise, and you will find it will work. Pain both physical and mental can draw your attention away. Your thoughts and body may seem to block your progress, but you can do it.

Undertake this relaxation exercise daily and make it a habit.

MISCONCEPTIONS AND FALSE VIEWS

The language we use can be misinterpreted. Sometimes the simplest things can be skewed and made to fit a preconceived idea. In the world of today, information is available at the touch of a screen, but much of it is propaganda or promotes opinions and views that are not built on solid ground. We all hold opinions that have been engraved into our psyche from our infancy to this day and in no way should you disregard it because you have been encouraged to follow the social norm, not that long ago it was thought smoking was healthy and up until 1986 corporal punishment was commonplace in UK schools. Others may tell you to believe this or that or give information contrary to your long-held beliefs, but hold firm because nothing is straightforward or black and white. Your true, or spirit self-understands deeper than language or concepts. There are many faiths all promoting their doctrine, but nearly all carry the two fundamental elements of love and forgiveness. Forgiveness of others is not condoning but understanding the act was performed through ignorance and a lack of consciousness and love. Ignorance is not meant as a derogatory expression; it applies to everyone until we reach a point in understanding. Forgiveness of others and ourselves is a stepping stone to understanding. If a child has a tantrum, you calm them and try to explain and forgive them because you know it is all part of growing up, and we are all in that process. The Christian, Jew, Muslim, Buddist, Hindu, Sikh and many other beliefs have their fundamentalists who want everyone to see what they consider as truth and sometimes take extreme action to reach that goal. Murder has been perpetrated in their cause, but in understanding, the true nature of life will show that to change your world you must first change yourself. We are constantly bombarded by concepts and teachings founded on false assumptions, but only through personal experience will you begin to see the truth. Your worldview will be totally different from mine, but both are true. When you open your self to the unseen world, you will find answers to all the questions you will ever ask. Words can be misunderstood as semantics can be an issue in any language. When I use the term Spirit, I could substitute it with God, Singularity, Cosmic self, Higher self, Divine Spirit or Superself. For me, all of these refer to the essence of the divine and every morning when you look in the mirror you see directly into the eyes of the divine. There are those who think that the world is controlled by the new world order while others believe it's extraterrestrials who manipulate us. Much of the misinformation has been passed on through social media as truth, but in developing your connection to your spiritual self, the truth will be shown to you. Consider that you are not insular, but an element of the cosmos; things do not just happen to you, you make them happen. Your life has been constructed by your thoughts and actions. The multi-millionaire looking out from his penthouse is no different to the beggar in the street below, both have made an impact and influenced the world that they know. They both have the capacity for love and compassion, and both born pure and unknowing, but through their actions, one has reached what many consider the top of the social order, and the other is someone to be avoided, but they are both living the best they can, yet in the eyes of the spirit-self, they are equal.

PERCEPTION

Mediums are normal with differing political persuasions, cultural backgrounds and beliefs. most believe in the angelic world and many in fairies, they are a mixed bag, but all have the ability to connect to another world or dimension. Many think that Mediums and Psychics are different, where Mediums connect directly to the spirit world, and Psychic get information from an energy field. It is also thought all Mediums possess a psychic ability, and not all Psychics have a mediumistic ability. However, my view is more straightforward. The Mediums and Psychic both receive information from a source not yet understood and only by making that connection yourself can you have an inkling of its nature. The spiritualists have a vast array of views. You only need to find four or five witnesses to an accident to find you have a few different versions of the same event. Even you and I will probably have some false memories. I know spiritualists who believe their spirit guide is Moses while some have a Native American and even I believe I have a spirit helper called Mat who was a Viking, who now prefers fishing to fighting. (spirit guides are considered as an entity that acts as a protector and guide to a human.) Then you have those who use ritual, but the list is endless with crystals and other tools being incorporated into the method of reading. There are numerous opinions and beliefs relating to this subject, for we create the world we inhabit, and when delving into the subject of the continuation of the personality after physical death, a concept that in our current incarnation is impossible to comprehend, we construct a scenario that makes sense to us. The way we perceive the connection to spirit is personal, and Spirit can only work with the material and tools available. The material is memory and experience and the tools your senses. If you've never known something spirit couldn't use it, as they use your memories and experiences to convey information. Spirit works with your imagination, and some of us have weird stuff locked inside our heads. Today's world is very different from that of one hundred years ago, and in one hundred years from now, it will be different again. In each era, perceptions will be very different. I often hear someone talk about the good old days, but we tend to forget the bad bits, and even I tend to romanticise things that were definitely not good.

I joked at an Open Circle that we could run a course for a reasonable fee, or maybe even a very large fee, and at the end, we would issue an accreditation certificate to prove the holder's ability, but in truth, organisations do exactly that. I had a string of letters after my name during my mid-career to help prove my competence as a designer when in truth the best proof was the quality of my last project. Accreditation sways perception not only for others but for the holder as well.

The view we hold of ourselves has been formed from our experiences and early years of development. When a child, Louise Hay was told she couldn't dance as she was too tall, but in her later years took ballroom dancing lessons. Other peoples views affect our perception of ourselves. So within the pages of this book lets break down all the negative views and perceptions we have of ourselves.

BRINGING MIND, BODY AND SPIRIT INTO ALIGNMENT STAGE TWO

In segment four we relaxed, and that's what I would like you to do again, but this time with two additions. First, you are going to use your imagination and create a glowing light emanating from your heart; then as your thoughts come and go pay attention to them. Be aware of them, even to the point of having paper and pencil by your side. However, don't react to your thoughts just observe. Relax by working up your body as before and visualise the tension leaving each part. Be aware of each section as before, but this time also imagines a light shining from the centre of your body, this is the white light of love and divine protection. (*I've already given an explanation about protection in the first section of this book and will expand on it later*). When you reach your head, jot down your thoughts. Do not worry if you don't manage it the first time; there's no rush, try again later. After this exercise goes for a brisk walk, this will bring your metabolism to its normal functioning state.

Body - Relaxing counteracts the chemicals you produce when you are under stress. Relaxation can help to reduce anxiety and depression, and it slows down brain wave activity. All in all relaxing is good for you.

Mind - As the body relaxes, the brain chemistry rejuvenates. Your brain is like the computer hardware your mind uses to interact with your surroundings, and you need yours in the best possible condition. Only when you are in a relaxed state can the mind pick-up information.

Spirit - Regardless of what your body and mind are doing your spirit is experiencing, but in relaxing, you are enabling your mind to interact with your spiritual self. Relaxation is something most do not do. You may come home from a hard day's work, grab something to eat and crash on the sofa to watch the television, but in doing that you could be watching something that will still elevate your heart rate and continue your creation of stress chemicals. Even if you can sit for a few minutes every day, your spirit will benefit from your connection.

We are not all equal. The social and geographical area you were born into, together with your upbringing helped form who you are. There can be a massive difference in consciousness and understanding between you and your neighbour. It should also be stated that genetic and physical conditions have an impact, yet neither is inferior or superior because both came into the world as a blank canvas. The misfit and genius have equality in the eyes of their spirit-selves.

If you are still reading this, you have made a conscious effort to try to understand yourself and the world around you. You want to improve your understanding, yet your spirit-self already understands. In relaxing, you will learn to listen to your inner voice. Take a closer look at the notes you made in the second relaxation exercise. If you look deep enough, you may find the answers to questions you have been asking.

SPIRIT AND THE PROCESS OF MEDIUMSHIP

A simplistic explanation of the mediumistic connection is that two spirits are communicating, one with a body and one without. This may sound over simplistic, and we all know nothing is straightforward. However, there are those who say the personality cannot continue after physical death and even more who think we shouldn't attempt to make the connection. Science has discovered how the brain works, and the function of neurotransmitters but at a subatomic level we are made of particles, and it is too simplistic to think of those particles as solid. So is it too much to consider it possible that a nonphysical part of yourself exists? Those who've developed the ability to make that connection, know the personality doesn't die with the body. How do we know that? Well, we can't Prove it as proof is defined as evidence, argument or action that establishes a fact or the truth of a statement. Or a series of steps in a resolution of a mathematical or philosophical problem. The Medium knows through his or her experiences during the process. A person may go for a reading occasionally, but a Medium who specialises in readings goes through the process again and again, and in doing so builds a body of evidence from positive validation. There will also be a body of negative responses. As I said, nothing is straightforward. Obtaining validation is important for a number of reasons, but the main one is to build confidence and to help in the interpretation of symbolic information. I will sometimes get the vision of a roundabout or carousel. This could refer to an actual place, but could also represent a situation that keeps repeating over and over again. To help build trust in what we are picking up, I have used a method in Circle that takes the following format:

Someone is designated to be the escort and take notes.

The person coming for the reading turns up a quarter of an hour before the Circle has started, When the sitter enters, those undertaking the reading are turned away from the sitter, the recipient has been instructed not to speak for the first fifteen minutes, band should respond to the escort with a nod or shake of the head. In the second fifteen minutes, the sitter can only respond with a yes or no. However, any reference to the sex or age of the sitter is rated as zero as audible clues can be obtained. Statements made by the Mediums that would give the recipient a choice and general comments that could be taken by the majority are marked as zero. All statements that could be positively validated are marked as one, and those that could not be taken are scored as a minus one but noted because they may relate to prediction. Then the marking ends, and the Mediums can turn and face the sitter, who can give an explanation if any is needed. Sounds tricky, but it's not. The last time this was done the result was

13 discounted or choice statements

51 positive

6 negative

For a thirty minute reading, it may not seem many statements were made, but those giving the reading tend to be certain before making any comment as they know it will be scored. Validation builds confidence. However, it can backfire if the sitter can't grasp what the Medium or spirit intend, or it may relate to a prediction. The medium, through practice, knows the information they are receiving is coming from somewhere other than visual, verbal or other physical means. Mediums experience something others cannot comprehend, but with training, anyone can make that connection.

In working with the unseen world the mind, body and spirit mingle with those in the spirit world (*Or whatever label you wish to place on it, as our current persona is unable to comprehend fully what this other existence is like*). The knack is, to differentiate between what thoughts are yours, and what are theirs.

The Body Of The Medium. - In the early stages of making the connection, there can be a tendency to feel overwhelmed or even uncomfortable. If this happens all that needs to be done is to tell the spirit to step back as the spirit world want the Medium to feel relaxed. I can find that I will start using gestures. I once kept tapping the inside of my lower arm, and it wasn't until the recipient told me, it was the act of looking for a vein to inject. (recipient or sitter, i.e. the person the reading is for). The Medium can also feel discomfort even pain, this is never overpowering but a way of drawing your attention to a part of the body. Spirit can only use your memories as a comparison. If you had never gone through a certain experience spirit could never expect you to convey the information.

It is no more than a spirit interacting with Spirit, one inhabiting a body, the other not.

PERCEPTIONS OF THE OTHER WORLD

Our upbringing has a bearing on the perception of our spiritual nature. The person raised in the Catholic faith compared to someone bought up in the home of New Age thinkers or atheist parents will be different, and none would be right or wrong. Our perception of the Spirit world or its nonexistence will have been formed by early teachings and trying to wipe away those deeply held thoughts would be a near if not impossible task. It's like being told not to think of a bright yellow elephant with red spots, and the first thing you think of is a yellow elephant with red spots. All those horror stories, old wives tails and urban myths build and form our opinion. So when I mention evil spirits and demon's, what pictures form in your mind? We all have thoughts locked deep inside. If you were raised as a Christian, you would have a view or opinion of the Devil, maybe even with horns and tail, but you and I have a preconceived idea. Then what of Heaven and Hell? There will be so much stored in your memory banks and once its there, it's there. As mentioned earlier I undertake Rescue Work, where I connect to a spirit that hasn't moved on. However, It's important to state that in all the time I've been doing this I've never encountered what I consider a demon. I've come across spirits who gave the appearance of being demons but in each case what appeared to be something so hideous was no more than a frightened, angry spirit that didn't or couldn't move on. Although we are blind to the true essence of the spirit world, from my connections, I feel once the spirit is free from the body and crosses to the other side evil no longer exists. Evil on the earth is due to a lack of consciousness and understanding. Our experiences will have built a picture of the Spirit world, and some of us, if confronted by something that appeared evil would probably run a mile thinking it had been dragged from the depths of hell. Perception can be an issue especially for those bought up with the notion of hell and damnation. If this is you, I would ask, if God loved you and created you would he be so cruel? I will answer that, not the God bit, as that will come later, but hell as a place does not exist. The simplistic explanation goes something like this: Existence on earth where we have free will, and there is a lack of true love can be hellish and for some pure agony and torment. Then we have the spirit world where there is only true love and understanding. However, wiping away all you've been told isn't the answer, as Spirit needs to use your thoughts to convey a message, and some of us have weird stuff in our minds. Mediums are only human and therefore imperfect, yet as dysfunctional as we are some of us still try to make that connection, for making it helps to bring understanding.

Body - Your physical location and era you were born, together with your upbringing has made you into the person you are today and will continue to direct your thoughts
Mind - Your thoughts create your perception.
Spirit - Is pure and is experiencing through your perception.

Mind, Body and Spirit are not separate, and one is not superior to the other.

PROTECTION

Do you feel you are placing yourself in a position of vulnerability if you love? The word love is glibly thrown around and encompasses a number of feelings, from the simplest of pleasures to complex emotions. However, the love I am referring to is more profound; it's love without limitations, it may be seen as unconditional, but add compassion and empathy. Well, this is what I do, and I believe others do when opening themselves to the spirit world, as the saying goes, 'when you walk a mile in someone else's shoes, you understand why they are like they are. If you're concerned about connecting to the other world, that concern will hinder the process, as your thoughts help to create your reality and the spirits perception of you. Let me take you back to basics for a moment. Spirit communicates with spirit, one with a physical body and one without. I help those stuck between the two worlds, and trapped spirits can create issues. However, this will never be a problem if you create thoughts of protection. Thoughts of protection will keep all issues away, as Louise Hay said, thinking positive thoughts will produce positive outcomes, and negative thoughts will bring negative results. In the middle ages, some individuals understood this very well, with the selling of amulets and spells for love, protection, good health, prosperity and much more. Even today some have a St Christopher necklace, four-leaf clover, or a lucky charm of some kind. Two Mediums who helped me during my early development had two different outlooks; one knew she was looked after totally by her spirit protectors, and the other just knew nothing bad could happen when she worked with the other world. Both were protected because disembodied spirits would see them as protected, strong and powerful. You can find gemstones are offered as protection from evil spirits, like agate, emerald, black tourmaline plus others, but once again it's not the crystal doing the work but the belief in the power of the stone. Other devices for protection are Holy water, or herbs like cumin, dill, clove. Burning sage is often used to remove evil spirits. In Circle, I use the following as an opening prayer. (a prayer is no more than talking and making a statement or affirmation:

"Divine Spirit surround me with the white light of Love and divine protection."

This puts the subconscious on the right path, and when working with Circles, I will sometimes undertake a short relaxation exercise to reinforce the belief further.

The script goes something like this:

(The group are usually seated).

Close your eyes.

Pause

Breathe as you would normally, do not try to control your breath.

Pause

As you breathe in, imagine you are inhaling the white light of love and divine protection, and when you breathe out, you are expelling all the dark negative energy you have accumulated.

Pause

Breathe in and relax

Pause

Breathe out.

Now visualise in the centre of your chest a bright glowing light.

Pause

And with each breath that light gets brighter and brighter.

Pause

With each breath the light fills your body, shining light onto every cell.

Pause

This light is pure and healing .
Pause
It is the light of love, the strongest element in this world and all others.
Pause
The light is now so in
tense that it radiates out from your core, shining like a beacon radiating love and protection .
Pause
That light will continue to shine, protecting you and all those you come into contact with.
Pause
In your own time, bring yourself back to the room and open your eyes.

That exercise reinforces the belief of protection, but the effect is more far-reaching, for when we connect to a spirit, we become entwined, we sense their emotions, feelings and visions, and they pick up ours. Therefore if a spirit that hasn't transcended connects, they see the light shining and understand the power the Medium has. The power is never held by an object or the act of ritual but in the person's belief. Not surprising mine is the same as my teachers. I am totally protected at all times and so are you if you believe. There are many guided meditations for spiritual and psychic protection, but these usually deflect an attack, leaving the troubled spirit to harass someone else, for that reason, I prefer to help find a resolution.

Mind - Believing you are protected is an opinion created through persuasion. Whereas having faith introduces trust which is stronger. So through the connection to Spirit, you will believe, but faith will allow you to protect others as well as yourself if you introduce love. Believe in your power of protection and have faith.

Body - Depending on your attitude of mind and location you are more likely to be attacked by someone walking on this planet than a nontranscendent spirit.

Spirit - The joining of the two worlds involves the intermingling of two spirits one with a body and one without. Spiritually you are indestructible.

THE CONNECTION

The Medium communicates with a consciousness of someone who once had a physical presence. they don't just pick up their memories, but feelings and emotions. The skill is not in making that connection but in differentiating between the Mediums feelings and spirits. The more the Medium connects, the more they understand. Imagine you've been invited to a gathering, it could be a birthday party or a formal function, but automatically you would behave in an appropriate manner. Well, the Medium has been invited to a gathering of spirit, and through compassion will do the same. Love, empathy and being nonjudgmental are vital. We are all dysfunctional, or put another way; we are like children, and from a lack of understanding we sometimes make bad choices. Spirit sees all, and although they've moved away from the material dimension, it doesn't mean they have abandoned those left behind. Some Mediums say they work through their spirit guides and others like me, except the information regardless. The connection is made, and the Medium receives visions and feelings both physical and emotional. Then there are bodily behaviours and hearing, rather like hearing the words in your head as you read. Sometimes the Medium senses their body is no longer their own, but every Medium experiences the connection in their own way, everyone is different. There is no right or wrong way, but the Medium needs to know that they are picking up information from Spirit, and not from visual or verbal clues because this only dilutes the validation.

Standing in front of a few hundred people and providing evidence of survival isn't for everyone, neither is giving readings, but working with spirit can help in your development.

Some Mediums, use this ability for their primary income so getting a good response is vital, but fraudulent activity has been reported. However, as I've already stated Mediums are only human, and when financial gain comes into play, I wouldn't be surprised if some have crossed the line to be deceitful. Trust and faith must be the cornerstone of all spiritual development. If you have taken or decide to take this path spirit will not let you down. Trust in them and have faith in your development, but building faith in the ability takes time. We all work differently, but regardless of how someone works, they need to ignore visual and verbal clues, as these will only act as a distraction. Also, the medium must resist the act of editing or making sense of what is being received. If I were scoring a reading for accuracy, I would ignore generalisations or choices, but in a reading situation, it is important to build the character of the personality coming through.

Mind - forget logic, and don't try to edit the information.
Body - Be relaxed and be aware of all physical sensations.
Spirit - Spirit connects with Spirit.

THE GARDEN OF EDEN

Your spiritual-self existed before you walked on this planet. I would like to use the allegory of Adam and Eve living in that beautiful garden, where everything was perfect. Other faiths have a similar story, but this one will do just fine. your spiritual-self existed in a place of perfection, just like the Garden of Eden, but perfection does not give the highs and lows that the game of life can provide. To taste the fruit from the tree or experience this life that is far from perfect; you must leave the garden of Eden. Yet we know nothing is straightforward or that simple. Imagine for a moment a garden that has many smaller ones hidden within it. You could turn a corner and be faced with a wonderful view or confronted by a door leading into a walled garden, then as you reach the far corner, behold is yet another, and as you move from one garden to another, a new plant would be discovered. The trouble with allegories is they can be taken literally. However, we may think we have been evicted from the garden by choice, but we have never really left. If we connect to this other world, we begin to see the bigger picture.

Spirit - Your spiritual-self exists in a state of bliss; it has chosen to experience life and to do this; it has allowed the formation of the ego and given it complete freedom, without prior knowledge of the unseen world. The ego is not separate from your spiritual-self, but a part of it.

Mind - Thoughts build our world, and the conscious element of ourselves is constructed by your surroundings, upbringing and genetic makeup. thought produces action, which ultimately creates. Every man-made product was bought into existence through thought. Even discoveries made by accident were further developed by the process of thought. Thinking leads to action that produces results. People who are optimistic are usually happier than those with a pessimistic outlook. Thought shape our world and positive thinking creates positive results, and negative thinking usually creates negative results. However, when the mind connects to Spirit, it leads to a better understanding of our existence.

Body - Your body should be in harmony with mind and spirit, as only at the point of physical death is the spirit free, but until then you function in the material world, and the body is used as a vehicle by which your spirit can experience this existence.

KNOW YOURSELF FIRST

Before we touch on connecting to Spirit, we need to be familiar with ourselves first. This relaxation exercise is simpler than the earlier one and is intended to make you familiar with how your body feels when it's in a relaxed state.

Relax and make sure you are comfortable. Your attention will be drawn to any discomfort, and you need to feel at ease.
Pause.
Be aware of your breath and the air moving in and out of your body. Don't try to control your breath just be aware of it.
Pause.
Visualise above your head an orb of white light, and with each breath, it gets drawn into your body.
Pause.
With each breath, the light shines brighter until the light permeates every cell of your body.
Pause.
Now be aware of how your body feels with the white light of love and divine protection radiating within and from it.
Pause.

Become aware of the surface of your skin from the tips of your toes to the top of your head. Note how you feel.

Pause.

If visions come into your mind pay it no heed, as you are only interested in your feelings, not sounds or imagery.

Pause.

Only be aware of where you are sitting and how it feels.

Pause.

Stay it this state for a time then open your eyes when you wish.

This meditation needs to be done for a few days; It will make you aware of your energy field, we all have one. Energy at a cellular level cannot be denied yet there is still a scientific debate regarding the existence of this electromagnetic field. You will find a lot of information about the Aura, but for now, put aside all thoughts as it is but a distraction, as we are only interested in sensing and getting to know how our body feels at this time. We perceive the world through our senses, sight, touch, sound, taste, smell, balance etc. but there is also the sense of inner knowing, and if you wish to connect to the spirit world you need to be able to differentiate between you and spirit.

Meditation is not difficult there's no need to sit in the lotus position or breathe in a particular way. You just need to be comfortable and relaxed. Thoughts will come and go, but if you see these thoughts as no more than your chattering mind trying to make sense of the world, you will begin to understand your true nature. You will find your attention being drawn to any distant sound and discomfort will be magnified as your mind will be drawn to it. Yet for now just be an observer and pay attention to how your body feels.

Meditation is an integral part of developing the mediumistic ability, but we don't want to be distracted by the process of meditation. I undertake guided meditations to help develop the connection to spirit, but being able to centre your self and know the difference between your thoughts and that of spirit, for now, is all that's needed.

Mind - Do not react to the thoughts, but observe.
Body - Be aware of how you feel physically
Spirit - Is happy to experience.

FORGIVENESS EXPANDED

To be truly relaxed and comfortable you need to dispel all feelings of anxiety, and one of the stumbling blocks is not being able to forgive yourself things you have done in the past. As we move through life, we do what we think is best from our understanding as it was then. Now we are different people. From your current state of consciousness, you understand that what you did was an error and no matter what you do now it can't be undone. It was in the past, and by rethinking, if only this, if just that, nothing can change what was done. You need to accept the error, learn from it and move forward. No one is perfect. Forgiving yourself is necessary for your spiritual growth. The church of Rome has the confessional, and to those who haven't been raised in the Catholic faith may seems odd, but it's important to forgive yourself.

Mind - The mind needs to be free from recalling old misdeeds. Reliving the mistakes of the past locks you in the past.
Body - The cells of the body are aware of your thoughts, so your thoughts need to be of future fulfilment, not that of reliving past deeds.

Spirit- Your spirit is undisturbed by past mistakes.

GOD

Always a tricky subject because people have deep-rooted views about God. Religious belief and the concept of God's, God or no God was placed in front of them from infancy. Mothers have sacrificed their children to appease the God's. Genocide has been committed to the belief that it was God's will. Nations waged War against nations with both sides feeling that God was on their side.

Is it God's will that a child is in pain through abuse or neglect. No, we have been given free will. As my father often said, "Hell does exist, and we are working through it". Humanity has shaped this world to its will, and it's a fragile place.

We'll all have an opinion on what is, or is not, but by whatever name you wish to use it's irrelevant, as knowing makes little difference to our existence. When we were bought into the world, we were complete and had nothing to compare ourselves to. You and I were perfect, and in essence, we still are. As babies, we weren't concerned with God or Gods or what we should or should not believe. The social order has shaped your thoughts, and there's no need for anyone to try to persuade any of us otherwise. Your belief is fine, and in a way, it's futile, as it's impossible to define the undefinable. One thing though, please don't think God will judge you as from what I've been shown there is only love and compassion that awaits us.

My perception of God goes something like this: The spiritual world doesn't adhere to the laws of physics as currently understood, but some use the idea of vibration. However, it's more complicated than that, although possibly the best way to describe it. So here goes: We function on a lower vibration, and the spiritual world operates at a higher vibration, and the highest vibration of all is the singularity or God that creates, but even my vision of God is irrelevant, just stand back and observe the world around you. The giant Oak that stands in the forest just exists and is unaware of any such concept. The dog that gives so much love doesn't give two hoots about God; they are just happy to run in the park and chase that ball.

Mind - So much time can be wasted by contemplating the form and existence of God.
Body - If God created everything it created your body and you have a duty to look after it.
Spirit - Your spirit is aware of the truth, and that in itself is enough.

DEVELOPMENT

Regardless of your progress, the destination is the same, but the journey can be made pleasant or unpleasant depending on the choices you make. I have confronted what most would consider evil when undertaking a rescue. These have been spirits tormented due to their lack of understanding. Many individuals go through life blind to the knowledge that there is a spiritual dimension. However, if you are still reading this, I would bet that you are open to the thought that the spirit world may be able to assist us. Imagine you are standing at the entrance of the maze. The sign on the door has THE MAZE OF LIFE written in big bold letters, and below written in the very small script are the terms and conditions:

On entering you must take a pill from the blue box marked FORGET

You will be issued with equipment that may not function perfectly, but it will probably dictate how you will travel.

The direction you choose is your responsibility.

There are no dead ends.

Turning back will be impossible.

There is only one exit.

You can never see around the next corner.

Only on exiting the maze will you be able to take the red pill from the box marked, Remember.

However, Spirit can assist and sometimes do. They can see further ahead with all the possible outcomes as looking above the maze is always better than being in it.

Mind - You have free will and can choose any avenue open to you.

Body - The direction you take will have an effect on your body.

Spirit - Is experiencing the maze.

YOU ARE PERFECT

Before you entered the maze, you were perfect and as you travel through you probably believe as my school report always said, COULD DO BETTER. However, the truth is you are still perfect. Never doubt that you are a fantastic individual capable of doing and experiencing anything, but you can also elevate yourself above the maze.

As you start to travel through the maze of life the social order will encourage you to react in a certain way, it will want you to contribute. However, by walking with Spirit, you can transcend the maze.

Mind - You are a perfect creator, and every thought leads to creation, be it good, bad or indifferent.

Body - Your body is yours to use for as long as you live, it is a biomechanical wonder that knows how to repair its self.

Spirit - Your spirit is perfection.

THE GENIE IN THE BOTTLE

Your spirit, or you could say, super-self, superconscious, higher self, spiritual self, soul, lifeforce. Language tends to get in the way sometimes, yet if you called a radish a grape, you couldn't make wine from it. Your spirit wants your physical self to have whatever it wants; it's the genie in the bottle waiting to grant your every wish, and you are not restricted to three. Language is a way of conveying a thought. Thinking provides an emotional and physiological response, watch an exciting film, and your heart rate will fluctuate as you watch the story unfold. You may ponder the outcome of an important meeting and place a negative or a positive spin on it, but let's assume you think of all the things that could go wrong. Ping! Your genie will do all in its power to grant your wish. Thought is your Genie for spirit is connected to the singularity or original source. Many teachers know this. Your status and your name will be forgotten as the sands of time cover everything.

Mind - What you think will be.
Body - Is a temporary vehicle
Spirit - Is the Genie in the bottle.

WHERE DO YOU BEGIN AND END

There is no such thing as empty space as the latest scientific thinking confirmes that there is no empty space around the nucleus of an atom. (*The electrons are a small part while the nucleus makes up the rest.*)   You may consider outer space to be a void, yet the space between celestial bodies is a vacuum containing plasma of hydrogen and helium and lots of other stuff. The physical world is energy, and the scientific establishment is still trying to understand its laws, but you cannot exist as an isolated entity, you are an integral part of the physical cosmos.   Your body is incredibly complex; it can heal its self, processes food regulates body temperature and keeps your heart pumping without you having to think about it. You influence the physical world, just by existing. In the sacred writings of Hindu text, the subtle body that is made up of the ego and mind controls the physical body. Then you have others who think we have seven bodies and others who say it's five. However, the truth is beyond our understanding, and trying to make sense of this is just a distraction. The future is in your hands, or to be more precise, in your thoughts. Your spirit is the genie waiting to grant your every wish.

No matter what your belief, I can tell you from the connection I have had to the nonphysical world you are more than a biological oddity that was conceived and will eventually perish and exist no more. However, connecting with your spiritual self, helps you understand that this existence is not exactly as the majority think. Your spiritual body has the ability to go beyond the physical and connect to a higher reality. So, to answer the opening title, where do you begin and end. You existed before you came to this physical existence and you will continue to exist long after your body has disintegrated and your name is forgotten.

Mind - Your mind is part of your spiritual self.
Body - Is a tempory vehicle for your spiritual self
Spirit - Will never perish.

UNDERSTANDING

Opening yourself to the nonphysical world can help you see physical death as no more than a door to another world, a step to be taken on a journey. Misinformation and misdirection stand at every corner. Some of us go through life trying to gain influence, power, fame or fortune but in doing so, we may miss the truth about the game of life where happiness, experiencing Joy, love and kindness are some of the primary elements. Power or adoration is what the ego seeks, and because we create what we want to make our own story, we need to be watchful about what we say and what we think. My story or my created truth is different from yours, and yours will be different from those around you but don't think we are isolated. Every day you affect those you come into contact with, your actions have consequences, some good and some not. You may have been bought up with the belief that what you have done in this life will be judged by God. However, my belief is a little different, but before I get to that let me place before you a few ideas. The billions of people walking this planet exist, this is not an illusion it is a truth. Each person is experiencing some of the multitudes of emotions open to us. Each is playing a part in their own story. There are millions of teachers out there trying to point us in the right direction, and some make a good living in doing so. They may tease you, by telling you what you can achieve, but your life cannot be summarised by achievements alone but by in experiencing and understanding all the emotions ranging from sorrow to happiness, and bliss to misery. The understanding of these emotions will set you free. We have all suffered mentally, some more than others, but by realising suffering is created internally by our thoughts we have a chance to alleviate or eradicate suffering. I love life and see the positive rather than the negative, but in the past, I have suffered. I felt a need to justify my actions. I wanted my art to be recognised and admired, and I had a need to be remembered long after my body had perished. *I know it's sad,* but that's before I started to work with the unseen world.

Experience and observation are key, but as I've said before our thoughts help build our reality. So when something happens that throws a negative situation at me, I use one of Louise Hay's affirmations. "OUT OF THIS SITUATION ONLY GOOD WILL COME,

AND I AM SAFE". I also ask Spirit to take the situation and deal with it. I hand it over and carry on with my story, knowing that Spirit will resolve it for the best result for everyone.   Understanding comes from observing not only our thoughts but the reaction of others. I live in the real world, and I am aware we all have issues and working as a Medium you open yourself to the full gambit of human emotions not only from the unseen world but from the recipient or sitter. Some people are so desperate to have validation about someone past, but it's never that simple. If I were to take onboard the suffering of others, I would have been strapped into a straight jacket and carried away by the men in white coats long ago. However, when I am working between the two worlds, I tend to see the bigger picture, sometimes seeing where the fear comes from. Some people want a reading from a Medium, again and again, desperate to have that experience. I may not approve, but this is where I need to stand back, as it's not my place to control or judge, but I do have a duty to guide.

Mind - Helps create our story

Body - The physical body is affected by your spirit

Spirit - Will deal with issues in a magical way

THAT OTHER PLACE

Let me state, you cannot describe the indescribable, a bit obvious I know, but it should be said before you read the next couple of paragraphs.

As soon as the lady walked in, I saw in my mind's eye a brick built humpback bridge spanning a canal. The reading was short, and the bridge was the main element. Validation was given because the description matched the location where she met her friend *(no longer with us)* most lunchtimes. So I know I was picking up information from the unseen world to pass on, but I wasn't getting any sense of what the nonphysical world was like, but I've been given snippets. Taking the earlier statement, and as a further example, let's assume you've never seen a Giraffe and one happens to be walking through an area where bushes hide the body and legs, and the trees obscure the head. Could you describe the animal? However, Spirit can give insight, like explaining to a child of four how they were conceived. So This is my take on the nonphysical world.

First, it's not up or down, but a state where the laws of physics as we know them, no longer apply.

Second, There are many plains of existence.
Third, Not everyone transcends immediately. Some can become stuck close to the material world
Forth, Spirit is eternal and plays the game of life to experience.
Fifth, We are not isolated from the spirit world, nor the spirit world from us.

The following is a short FICTIONAL story:

Subdued light came from the nurse's station, and the ward was quiet except for the occasional snoring from the lady in the end bed. The figure standing a few feet away was wearing white with a lovely set of wings and blond hair. If he'd been sent to help Merinda, Mat would have appeared differently; aboriginal spirits don't need wings, and white skin and blond hair would not have been appropriate. Her breathing was becoming laboured; then as the last breath left, Rose floated out of the body she'd been using for the last ninety-five years. Rose wasn't surprised to be confronted by this beautiful angel, as she knew he was standing there days before. With a kind smile, Mat said,
" I'm here to help you", and offered her his hand, as their fingers touched Rose felt as fit

as a fiddle, no longer in pain, then glancing at her reflection in the ward window she was sure she looked more like 30 than 95, and the dress looked just like the one worn to that dance all those years ago. They both smiled, and when Rose looked away from Mats beautiful blue eyes, she noticed they now stood on lush green grass that made her think of her mother, and at that moment she was no longer holding Mat's hand, but the hand of her mother, looking exactly as she remembered her.

Okay, I think you get the drift.
Heaven is not up there, and Hell is not down there, in fact, Hell is another issue entirely.

Mind - Is unable to comprehend the nonphysical fully as we have no recall of a comparison.
Body - Is a tempory vehicle
Spirit - Is eternal

HELL

I have touched on my thinking about the subject of hell earlier, but my view is that you will not be judged and if found unworthy thrown into a fiery pit to suffer for eternity. We are all capable of taking the wrong road. If you accept the premise that we are spirit and therefore part of the divine, you must understand that the divine is ultimately pure love, and for now beyond our comprehension. Understand that God, pure Spirit, the Divine or whatever badge you want to pin on it, knows that we will eventually discard the ego. We've all digressed because we are human and learn through making mistakes. The language used by the great spiritual teachers of the world was intended to resonate with the time in which it was imparted. However, many of the teachings have been misinterpreted through translation and the passage of time, bastardised and twisted to manipulate the masses. We have free will, and the actions we take are down to a number of factors, genetic makeup, social programming, parental influence, schooling, physical ability and location are but a few. We pick up information as we move through life and react differently depending on our understanding. Some are spiritually aware and others not, but we create our reality through our thoughts.

There are billions of us walking this planet, and free will makes it a constant place of dark and light. Some seem to live a charmed life and others in hell. Regardless of the many factors that have led you to where you stand today, you can find at the flick of a switch or the press of a button an endless stream of pain and suffering. So hell does exist, but it isn't somewhere you will be cast forever by a God figure who will stand in judgment. Hell can be found around every corner if we wish to go there, but we can protect ourselves, with the help of our true spiritual self as this is stronger than our ego. By living in a world where we are constantly reacting rather than tapping into our intuition or inner understanding places us firmly in the world of the ego. However, by going inward, we can observe rather than react. If at the point of physical death a person has been so wrapped up in the world of the ego, it can result in them not progressing on their journey, and they become trapped *(as mentioned earlier)*. So hellish experiences may exist, but it's only temporary.

Mind - The mind can help us go within
Body - The body can assist the mind
Spirit - Spirit can provide the truth of a situation.

HOME

Make yourself comfortable close your eyes and relax, and be aware of your chattering mind and see the constant flow of thoughts and feelings. Notice them come and go, but don't dwell on them just observe. Then say to yourself, "I am safe, and home", for your body is a tempory home to your spirit. As a Medium, I'm constantly confronted by the effects of physical death. However, have you ever considered what it would be like to live in your body forever? One day science may well be able to repair and replace parts of our bodies that cease to function properly, but even in a few hundred years from now, if that was made feasible, being able to avoid death is not guaranteed. I love life and enjoy every second, but I know that the death of my body is certain. Okay, my ego doesn't want me to think about it, and will do everything in its power to stop me, but I have opened myself to the unseen world, so I know that living in this body is one step on a much longer journey. Mediumship has helped me to quieten the ego and connect to a deeper spiritual understanding. However, for now, we inhabit our bodies a biomechanical wonder. Even if it's in a state of disrepair and you're suffering, the spiritual element can help.

If the home you live in is unloved, it shows. How it looks is a reflection of you, if you don't empty the bin and let rubbish pile up or let the paint peel, it shows a lack of love. So first things first, love yourself. You are not unloved or alone; you are an eternal spirit. Looking after the body is something, we should all do, but If you don't love yourself, things will start to go wrong. Loving and respecting yourself is one of the many keys to a healthy and happy life, but it's not easy for as you try your ego kicks in.

Why bother.

Tomorrow will do.

What's the point, etc.:

It's now you need to balance and bring your spirit into focus, even if you are feeling unwell say to yourself.

"I love my body, and it knows how to heal itself. New healthy and vibrant cells are forming every second. My dis-ease will be replaced by vibrant health."

I know it sounds odd to say something like that when you feel so bad, but say it and believe it. Dwelling on illness does you a disservice. Think and act healthy as much as you can, for your mind is more powerful than you know.   Louise 1 Hay suffered from terminal cancer, in the mid-1970s and used her system of love and forgiveness to cure her dis-ease. She left this life at the age of 90 in the morning of August 30th, 2017.   Ridding yourself of anxiety, mental stress and negative thought have a positive effect on your body. So you need to give time to yourself, pamper and spoil yourself. You are not selfish; you are doing what you should. Yes, we will all leave this planet at some stage, but for now, you inhabit your body, and it needs to be loved. So cherish, spoil, and look after it the best you can, for that is your true home.

Mind - The mind can help create a wonderful home full of positive thoughts
Body - The body is the temporary residence for your spirit
Spirit - Spirit is happy to be.

OWNERSHIP

The world of the human is ego driven, where possession is an expression of power and wealth. We come into this existence naked and possessing nothing except the body we have been born into. Then we leave, discarding the body that has been our home for as long as we have resided on the earth. However, we do leave it with an abundance of experiences. Physical objects are part of that process, but if possessions become the focus, your world can fall apart. You never own anything, all you have is on loan, for when you leave the planet, everything will be left behind. What would you rather do, fill a shed with stuff or create experiences? Taking a holiday can be costally, but once taken those memories and feelings are retained by your spirit, and some memories can be priceless, but you didn't own the hotel, but you did experience the happiness felt. My passion is creating contemporary art, and I become lost in the process of creating, and when the work is complete, I will either sell it or give it away. For me, the excitement is in the creation of the object, not in its ownership. Yes I still have pictures dotted about the house, and I love looking at them, but I also love going to galleries. I will publish what I am writing then I will no longer own it. Hopefully, you will take what I have written and use it, built on it and do a better job than me. You will know when you have taken steps to join mind, body and spirit, as your attitude towards things will change, you will become more interested in experiences and feelings. You are a custodian of all you possess. You may have finished paying for your mansion, but one day you will pass it on to someone else. Do not get the impression that I am saying possession is a bad thing, as with possessing comes responsibility. How many stately homes have fallen into disrepair and who pays for the upkeep. We will all have different views, but I try to have a minimalist approach. If you see something you want and can afford it bye it. Enjoy life and the experience that possession can provide. There are two brothers I know, both very well off, and not short of a bob or two. One paid for his classic Bugatti, and the other given one by a lady who wanted someone who would love it as much as her husband had. The only stipulation was that he should never sell it. Things demonstrate wealth, and I will touch wealth in the next segment. However, do not become a hoarder, be like the lady left with her husbands Bugatti, pass things on, sell or give them away. All things have energy. even the smallest object, as someone invested effort into it. It was designed and produced, and that energy should not be locked away.

Mind - Notes and processes the experience.
Body - Is used to experience.
Spirit - Your spirit will retain the feelings and memories for eternity.

WEALTH

I consider myself to be one of the wealthiest people walking this planet, for I am healthy, fit, happy and enjoy life, love my work and the people around me. As for the money, it's always there when needed. My attitude towards life is different from many. Now I am a fan of the National Trust, a UK charity preserving historic places and spaces. They are open to the public for a fee but do I want a country mansion, NO! just think of the work and responsibility needed to keep it in order. I can only sleep in one bed, and I can be just as comfortable in a smaller room sitting in a cosy chair as I can in a grand sitting room with high ceilings. I appreciate the skills of the craftsmen who built, decorated and tended the house and gardens. However, the lord and lady of the manor were in many cases imprisoned by their wealth and social standing.

To be truly wealthy is to have the freedom to do what you want when you want. Okay, we are subject to social and moral standards, and stepping outside those constraints could land us in prison. So a limited amount of control is unavoidable, but I do expect some control. Most drivers follow the basic rules of the road, so keeping safe is relatively easy. I love the day job and never mind going to work, in fact, I love it, and as they say, if you enjoy what you do it never feels like work. You may see wealth differently. Maybe you see it as having residences around the world owning a private jet and so much money you can buy anything. If that's your preference, think about it and assume you have waved a magic wand, and hey-presto you have everything, but. *(Now, you knew there was going to be a BUT)*, can you generate true friendship, abundant health and happiness? Your ego will be worried that someone else will steal it or something will happen, and it will all be lost. Also, it takes management to handle that amount of stuff. Now make a wealth list including health, love, friendship and happiness, in with money the penthouse and all the other stuff, I bet health and love would be at the top.

I love my life, but things don't always go to plan, and when they don't I use one of Louise Hay's affirmations and say, I am safe and only good will come out of this situation. I just add one other action I still my mind and ask Spirit to deal with the situation and resolve it, so it works out for the best for all concerned. Then I move forward and trust those in the unseen world to do what needs to be done. It works!

I understand where my attitude towards money has come from, as in the past I've seen money as an issue not that it's been scarce, but I have never seen it as energy to be used. My grandfather was a butler and in charge of all the households and staff, and I've been told a number of stories about him. There is one about when he was walking the Earls pet dogs, and he passed a family being evicted from one of the many properties the Earl owned. With the children and few possessions on the pavement, he looked at the pampered dogs and in that moment changed his attitude away from capitalism, and worked in secret for the trade union movement leaning more towards communism. The other was more of a throwaway comment; Grandfather told my dad when the Earl went out the front door with one of his best suits on he went out the back wearing the other

Up till this point, I have always seen capitalism as fundamentally defective, but now I see money as energy that needs to be kept flowing. Money in its self-has no value it is an I.O.U. you can not eat it, you could use the paper to start a fire, but paper notes are fast being replaced. Money needs to be used, not hoarded under the bed. If you like me have had issues with money, affirm this:

The views and opinions of those in the past have no power over me, and I except the abundance of money that is rightfully mine.

I now expect money to flow towards me, but wealth is not just about finance it is much more than that.

Mind - The mind and thought can facilitate wealth
Body - The body needs to be healthy to experience wealth
Spirit - Spirit is wealthy

THE GIFT

How many times have you come across a Medium who has referred to their ability as a gift? In a way, it is, but it's a gift we've all been given. Both the beggar sitting in the rain and the millionaire in the penthouse have the ability, but will they want to develop it? However, you are still reading this which indicates that you are already using this skill or wanting to develop or understand it further. So for those who have untied the bow and unwrapped the gift and started to read its instruction, and for those of you who are already using this amazing ability, don't waste it. You will come across those who will tell you that you are doing something wrong or you need to do this or that. Listen but remember you are spirit residing in the physical world, so you are capable of connecting to that part of you that is all knowing. So if you ask and take time to listen; you will be given the answer. The gift is not the ability, but coming to an understanding or reaching a state of consciousness where you unwrap it, read the instructions and start to use it.

Mind - The mind already possesses the ability

Body - The body needs to relax
Spirit - Spirit already knows

OPEN OR CLOSE

I have included this note as I thought it might be of interest.

After a Circle, I will close the connection by grounding everyone, but what is right for one may not be right for another, as in the words of Frank Sinatra "I did it my way." I've decided there is work for me to do, so as from today I will not ground and close myself any more. I hear what some will say, but the spirit world will not let me burn out or send me flying off with the fairies. Every morning before I get out of bed I lie still and prepare myself for the day. I ask the spirit world to help and say to myself. "Today will be a happy day full of magic and wonder". I understand I need to function in the physical world, and as soon as I concentrate on a task that needs my attention the connection fades so I can focus. I know the unseen world can guide and assist in the simplest of tasks and remaining open can be useful.

Mind - The mind needs to be still.
Body - Needs to be free from stress.
Spirit - Spirit is always free to connect.

YOU

You are a pure spirit a soul or nonphysical entity inhabiting a physical body, and the spirit part of you is unaffected by the laws of the material world, but able to experience it through the physical body. You have free will, but it's influenced by your personality that has been shaped by your life experiences. So when you come across someone void of empathy consider how they came to be. It may be down to a flaw in the brain, or upbringing. We are all different, but understanding why people fall short in no way condones their actions. We are all responsible for what we do, but at some stage, we all leave this world and move on. It's hard to understand why some have the desire to kill, yet it happens all the time. Now put aside your thoughts about others, and turn inward, for you are at a stage where you see the world and life a little differently. The realisation that your thoughts shape your world can be a bit disconcerting, but the decisions you made in the past have been influenced by previous experiences. So from this moment on, your higher-self or spirit-self can assist in all decisions if you wish. Acknowledge the errors made in the past and put them behind you, for they were made from your understanding at that time. Sit down by yourself and write your affirmation slowly and consider each letter and word as the pen or pencil flows across the paper. Your higher-self understands everything because your spirit is eternal, and your Spirit will guide, support and keep you safe. As mind, body and spirit become balanced you see life anew; standing back to see situations outside the influence of the ego. Life is a journey, and some see the signposts along the way, while others rush past as they feel there's a lack of time, where in fact the opposite is true, for you are a spirit and will exist for eternity. If you have never been shown love how can you give it, and would you expect the same behaviour from a child of six as you would from an adult? Forgive yourself and don't expect to be perfect, as that's an impossible task. Your true-self is experiencing this existence regardless of whether you have developed spiritually or not, but if you have a better understanding of your true nature, you can use it to your advantage in this manifestation. So no matter what you have done in the past put it to one side, or even better, throw it in the spiritual trash can, and ask the spirit world to deal with it, for you can not be blamed for doing something you didn't know shouldn't be done. We are all children in the eyes of the divine, but although society attempts to govern with compassion, it still feels there is a need for punishment. However, the true nature of the spirit world only forgives, never condemns. A child hasn't the capability to understand fully so would you sentence a girl of six to death for taking the life of another child? I think not for you know they were not fully aware and still needed time to mature. You inhabit a biomechanical body and can abuse it or take care of it. You may think you have decided what to do, but your decisions have been influenced. However, regardless of your past, you have the power to change. Your past is not the present, and what you do this very second helps determine your future. So be watchful of your actions and thoughts for they can either in prison or set you free.

Mind - Needs to let go of any self-criticism
Body - Can be helped or healed by the spirit
Spirit - Understands and forgives everything.

CLOSING COMMENT

Any doubts I had about the continuation of the personality after physical death have long been dissolved, but if you've not had the experience of a direct connection it would be hard to comprehend, but regardless of your life experiences, you will come to your own conclusion. However, it has no influence on the day that you discard your physical body as the believer and nonbeliever will have the same outcome. Developing this ability has helped me on a practical level, and I hope that the act of writing this will assist you as much as it has helped me. I wrote this to assist in taking the Open Circle, but it then took on a life of its own helping me to resolve several issues. Communicating with the nonphysical can help heal the mind and body, but your spirit is perfect and needs no assistance,

THE END. (Although there is no end.)

Further publications by Derek Murray:

HOW TO BE A MEDIUM

A STUDY IN RESCUE MEDIUMSHIP

THE KEY THE DRAGON SLEEPS

OPEN CIRCLE NOTES.

BEFORE YOU GO, COULD YOU PLEASE
REVIEW THIS BOOK ON AMAZON AND
GOODREADS?

Thank you

Derek

Printed in Poland
by Amazon Fulfillment
Poland Sp. z o.o., Wrocław